TANGLED DESTINY

TANGLED DESTINY

France, Europe and the Anglo-Saxons

Roger Woodhouse

Thumbnail Publications

Published in Great Britain by
Thumbnail Publications
Sutton Coldfield

Copyright © Roger Woodhouse 2006

ISBN 0-9550223-1-2

All rights reserved. No reproduction, copy or
transmission of this publication may be made
without written permission.

Roger Woodhouse has asserted the moral right
to be identified as the author of this work.

Printed and bound in Great Britain by
Lamberts Print & Design
Settle, North Yorkshire

CONTENTS

PREFACE

ONE: EUROPE PAST AND PRESENT
The long view	1
The life and times of Jean Monnet	2
The Common Market	21

TWO: A LIBERAL INTERPRETATION
A rude awakening	27
A sense of history	32
Us and Them	39

THREE: THE POST-WAR WORLD
Pax Americana	45
A certain idea of Europe	50
After the Wall	59

FOUR: A TIME TO CHOOSE
The French exception	65
Of men and markets	78
Old habits	83
Freedom and democracy	105

NOTES

PREFACE

One year has elapsed since the referendum in France that rejected the European Constitution. In that period there has been a noticeable shortage of constructive suggestions about what the implications might be. In Britain the reaction has been mostly one of relief in political circles and indifference from the public. Yet something both important and strange occurred in May 2005. For half a century and more France was a prime mover in a process of European unification that Britain joined belatedly and, it was generally thought, half-heartedly. Curiously, therefore, the No campaign in France made much of the claim that the new Europe in prospect was liberal in inspiration and thus "Anglo-Saxon" by implication. Meanwhile, in Britain the same project seemed suspiciously continental in flavour. This short essay is an attempt to throw some light on the apparent paradox.

ONE

Europe Past and Present

The long view

History is made up of long cycles and brief episodes. Human lives are lived and great events occur on those bumps and curves. With the passage of time, we can look back and separate the trivial from the momentous, the enduring from the ephemeral. The longer the perspective, the more system and order we can perceive. The thousands who died on the Somme in 1916 did not know that they were fighting in the First World War. Likewise, the hostility between East and West that dominated the latter half of the twentieth century and brought the world to the brink of nuclear holocaust is now just another item on the curriculum. Who would have thought it?

Similarly, when we look at Europe today we are adrift somewhere between current affairs and contemporary history. European unification has now been in progress for more than half a century, and breaking news has necessarily to be understood in that context.

We are not yet in a position to draw a line under the whole enterprise and dissect everything with the benefit of hindsight. That day may or may not come; in the meantime we must put things in place as best we can. In May 2005 a referendum in France rejected the European Constitution that was supposed to mark the latest stage in an ongoing process to forge a common destiny for the peoples of Europe. Why did that happen and where does it leave us?

Accepting that no definitive answer is possible, we can still attempt an interim appreciation of the significance of that rejection. Until all is said and done, any point of departure must be to some extent arbitrary. Nevertheless, the sort of Europe we have today is associated above all with the name of one man. We can begin with his story.

The life and times of Jean Monnet

Jean Monnet was born in Cognac in 1888 and grew up in a family that was naturally open to the outside world. His father's brandy business regularly brought to their home visitors from America, Germany or Scandinavia. Monnet's earliest memories were of these guests enjoying the hospitality of his mother's table and talking of their home countries, their travels and events around the world. In these convivial surroundings the young Jean learned that common goals make common interests and that even relationships of an essentially economic nature can be honest and human. This outlook on life was reinforced later during his visits to clients in Canada during the first decade of the twentieth century, where he found new arrivals from Europe moving into what were still wide open spaces. What struck Monnet was the matter-of-fact spirit of co-operation that joined people together where plentiful natural resources were equally available to all.

Over the years that followed, Monnet's travels took him as far afield as the United States, Russia, Sweden and Egypt. It was the understanding for international business that he developed during this period that brought him into public life on the outbreak of the First World War. Monnet quickly saw that this would be a conflict in which economic forces would be as decisive as military power. For this contest of production and supply, Germany had the advantage of running a unified operation, whereas Britain and

France each made their own arrangements, resulting in duplication and inefficiency. Worse still, they were competing with each other for materials purchased on world markets and so driving up the price. Monnet's solution was for the efficient flow of essential goods to be made the responsibility of joint Anglo-French councils.

In those days, the notion that two allies might combine their buying power appeared an outlandish proposition. It was one thing to send young men to die in the same mud for the same cause, but to open the purchase ledger to foreign eyes seemed almost like treason. The fact that a young man with no political experience was able to establish just such a system was a tribute to Monnet's powers of persuasion in two languages. For the duration of the war, the necessities of life in Britain and France such as cereals, sugar and meat were obtained on this joint basis. The responsibility of the state for the welfare of its citizens thus became part of a broader context encompassing the needs of men and women in another country.

When the war was over, Monnet served as deputy secretary general to the League of Nations until 1923, when he returned to the family business. Duty then called again in 1939 on the outbreak of a new war against Germany. In June 1940 he convinced Winston Churchill that the desperate struggle in which the two countries were involved required no less than the complete merging of Britain and France into one Anglo-French Union. It was too late, however, and France was overrun before the fusion of the two nations could be ratified. Because that historic step was never taken, Monnet remained purely and simply a French citizen, but nevertheless went to Washington as a British civil servant with the important task of mobilizing the industrial capacity of the (still neutral) United States to supply the war effort.

With the return to peace in 1945, Monnet retained the same philosophy that essential materials should be distributed according to where they were needed rather than where they happened to be found. Where this cut across frontiers or clashed with the prerogatives of the nation-state, an appropriate organization needed to be set up to bridge that divide. This was the principle behind the European Coal and Steel Community, which laid the first foundations for the

European Union as we know it.

It is thanks to Monnet, therefore, that we can look back on a process of European integration spanning more than half a century and culminating in the EU of today. Because of one man, European history took the course that it did. From Monnet's perspective, however, the years to come were overshadowed by a single question that demanded a really good answer if the future was not to be a dreadful repeat of the past. First and foremost, the Coal and Steel Community solved the problem of what to do about Germany.

In Hitler's war, German heavy industry based on coal and steel had again been crucial in supplying the military hardware required to contend for world domination against the British Empire, the United States of America, and the Soviet Union. After a hard-won victory, these allies set about dismantling Germany's steelworks so that they could never again be used as an arsenal of war.

That policy had to be revised when the Iron Curtain descended across Europe, splitting Germany into East and West. In the Cold War, the industrial heartland of the Ruhr valley found itself on the side of the "free world". These particular Germans were now our friends and allies; it made no sense to destroy their livelihoods and deprive the western democracies of a valuable asset. The metallurgical sector which was the bedrock of the West Germany economy therefore had to be revived.

Such was the reality of the situation. To the French, however, this was cold comfort. For France, the war had been a crushing defeat followed by a long and humiliating occupation. The idea of even apparently rehabilitated Germans again flexing their industrial muscles was a worrying prospect. Nor was it just the possibility that one day those foundries and forges would once more turn out weapons for another invasion. Even in peacetime, French industry could not prosper with West Germany as a commercial rival. France's programme of post-war recovery had not planned for a return to open competition and was therefore doomed to failure as soon as the furnaces of the Ruhr were again operating at full capacity. What was needed was a way to get West Germany back to work while providing an assurance that this would not pose a threat to France, either militarily or economically.

At heart the question was about managing the relationship between a country blessed with plentiful natural resources, and its less fortunate neighbour. It was reasonably clear to all concerned that the problem would require something like the typical Monnet approach. Speaking to the British Ambassador in February 1948, the President of the French Republic, Vincent Auriol, even used a favourite example of Monnet's when he evoked the Tennessee Valley Authority in the USA as a model of the sort of organization that might be set up to ensure that the industries of the Ruhr were run for the benefit of Europe as a whole.[1]

In May of that year, a member of the British government gave his opinion. As minister with special responsibility for Germany, the Chancellor of the Duchy of Lancaster, Lord Longford, felt strongly that any control of the Ruhr must lead on to, and become merged with, a general integration of European resources. Longford was convinced that in the years to come anything less would be resented by a new generation of Germans as unfair discrimination. The only answer was for the same control to be extended to every country in due course.²

Back in France, the British Embassy in Paris was hearing views from another part of the political spectrum. Vincent Auriol was a Socialist, whereas Léon Noël was a member of General de Gaulle's inner circle. In November 1948, Noël outlined the idea of an equal partnership between the Ruhr and the industrial area of France in the Lorraine basin as part of an integrated Western European plan. He was, however, vague about how this might be achieved.³

Thinking along the same lines but equally unsure how to proceed in practice was the diplomat who would within a few weeks be named French High Commissioner in Germany, André François-Poncet. In December 1948 he also was convinced that control over the Ruhr had somehow to be integrated into a broader Western European system. In his mind this might be organized something like an international cartel which would allocate production programmes to its members. In this way Germany would be on an equal footing but would still be subject to regulation.⁴

All of these musings on the problem prefigured in

a general way the eventual solution but remained nothing more than ideas in the air until a definite plan to pool French and German coal and steel resources was announced on 9 May 1950. Only at that moment did Monnet produce the something extra that would transform a patchy consensus about what might perhaps be done into a real basis for action. The added ingredient was the High Authority, to which both countries (and any others that chose to join) would yield their sovereignty where these two key industries were concerned. Until this moment, the ideas in circulation had assumed that any organization set up would provide for decisions to be taken between nations. The High Authority meant that those decisions would in fact be taken at a level above the nations that became members. The change from international to supranational took Europe across the threshold of a new era.

At this moment, however, there was no such thing as a "Community". There was one idea and one institution. Together they did all that was required at the time. As usual, Monnet's answer was the rational organization of resources under the guidance of a group of individuals with everyone's best interests at heart. That technique was now being pushed to new limits and, in the name of the common good, the High Authority would deal with matters that had traditionally been the business of national governments. In one sense, the plan unveiled in May 1950 was therefore just a variation on the familiar Monnet method. On the other hand, a taboo was being broken and things would never be the same again between France and Germany, nor in Europe as a whole.

But where would this lead? The official announcement read to the press by the French Minister for Foreign Affairs left no doubt – the coal and steel organization would be the first step towards a European Federation.[5]

This was an ambitious claim in the circumstances. As the words were being spoken it was not known how many other countries would join the scheme nor how it would work in practice. Except for the High Authority, every last detail remained to be decided. On this one point, however, Monnet was absolutely inflexible. The rest was open to discussion, but unconditional acceptance of the principle of supranationality was the price for a seat round the table where the technicalities would be worked out. This is what France and West Germany had agreed and they would not budge. Even the British, who were generally Monnet's preferred working partners, were told to take it or leave it.

In the event, Britain chose to leave it. The countries that did accept were France, West Germany, Belgium, Luxembourg, the Netherlands and Italy. This was the fateful moment when the "Six" went one way and Britain the other.

To see it in those terms, however, does rather raise the question of what direction the "Six" were heading in. Given that Britain has ever since been cast in the role of a reluctant European, it seems fair to ask exactly what it is she is always lagging behind. Is a European Federation actually under construction? Is that really what has been happening since the day in May 1950 when the announcement of the coal and steel pool held out that prospect with such apparent certainty. Perhaps the greatest obstacle to understanding Europe in the first decade of the new millennium is that after so long the answer to this simplest of questions remains very much a matter of taste.

Let us be clear. There is no doubt that in the aftermath of the Second World War there were those who believed in a federal future for Europe. For example, the Italian politician Altiero Spinelli made an impassioned speech to that effect at the founding congress of the Union of European Federalists as early as August 1947.[6] Nor was he alone. Across the continent, statesmen of the first rank were calling for the same thing. The wording of the declaration of May 1950 thus chimed nicely with the spirit of the age. What was not explained, however, was how the coal and steel pool and the promised federation were cause and effect. Nor does there seem to have been any definite plan in the mind of Jean Monnet himself beyond a determination to seize the moment.

The key chapter in Monnet's memoirs describes how the text of the now famous statement was arrived at.[7] This went through a number of versions, each meticulously drafted for clarity and maximum impact. Monnet and his team took it for granted that they were dabbling with a conception of Europe that was ultimately federal in nature. Against that background, however, the overriding concern was to take urgent and decisive action to defuse an impending clash of French and German interests in the field of heavy industry. The result therefore invited a federalist interpretation but its actual substance consisted of a reorganization of materials, labour and investment in line with the needs of the time. In this respect it was classic Monnet.

The coal and steel plan did, however, seem to carry connotations that lent a new aspect to the familiar style. Even seasoned observers were not quite sure what to read into this. A few weeks after the launch of the project, two civil servants in key economic posts on either side of the Channel had a long and confidential conversation. The Frenchman, Robert Marjolin, had worked closely with Monnet and knew him well. The Englishman, Eric Roll (later Lord Roll), asked him why he thought that Monnet had espoused the federal principle. Marjolin replied that he was not at all sure that in fact he had. He had espoused a new idea and probably did not care what the consequences were.[8]

Obviously Marjolin did not mean that Monnet was indifferent to the success or failure of the coal and steel plan in its immediate objectives. Marjolin was, however, very sceptical about the idea that the practical arrangements put in place to regulate the production and distribution of these commodities would start a process leading to the establishment of a federation as a matter of course. For him, the federalists were calling for a leap of faith that would leave Europe adrift in search of a dream. It was not that he found the notion of a European Federation unattractive. He just did not think that it was realistic. In his own memoirs he wrote that he would himself be a federalist if only he could believe that the goal was actually attainable within the foreseeable future. For Marjolin, vision, hope and optimism were not enough to transform Monnet's latest brainchild into any such thing.

Nevertheless, it did for a while seem that some of the components of an eventual federation were falling into place according to a natural progression. From the basic idea of the coal and steel pool grew the European Coal and Steel Community. From "pool" to "community" was not just a symbolic change of name. The founder members had fleshed out the institutional structure so that the High Authority was flanked by a Common Assembly and a Council of Ministers.

The former was a gathering of delegates from the parliaments of the "Six". The latter consisted of members of the national governments. The new "Community System" thus stretched from a supranational element above the state, through the state itself at ministerial level and then to the citizens within each state via their elected representatives. In a very rudimentary fashion it did therefore occupy the same sort of political space as a federation.

To one way of thinking, if further Communities could be set up to handle other transnational matters on the same basis, a moment would arrive when the accumulated attributes of a federation would need only the name to be complete. All that was required was a series of problems to which a supranational solution could be applied, and a federation would eventually come about as an inevitable consequence.

The first such problem in fact presented itself even as the Coal and Steel Community was coming into being. Once again it involved the rehabilitation of West Germany among the European nations. How could West Germany contribute to the defence of democratic Europe against the threat from the communist bloc without raising an army of its own? The answer was a European Defence Community (EDC) complete with a European army in which German soldiers would serve. This would be more reassuring than the formation of an autonomous German army so soon after the war.

Monnet and his team began work on the new proposal, and the treaty establishing the EDC was signed by representatives of the six countries of the Coal and Steel Community in May 1952. It only remained to be ratified by the national parliaments. In the meantime it seemed clear that the next step would be a European Political Community with the authority actually to deploy the European army wherever and whenever necessary. Work began on a draft constitution with this in mind. This envisaged a parliament of two houses: a directly elected House of the People, and a Senate composed of nominees from national parliaments. The Community system, barely two years old, was moving rapidly towards the goal of a federation.

That process came to an abrupt halt, however, when the French parliament refused to ratify the EDC treaty in August 1954. It seemed that there could be, after all, a limit to the readiness of a nation-state to dissolve itself into a unified Europe. To cede control of heavy industry to a High Authority was one thing, but the European Defence Community would have meant the end of the French Army, together with a certain idea of France graven in stone on a thousand monuments to a glorious past. The treaty was rejected without even a debate.[9]

This was a double blow to a method of European unification that relied on tackling the burning issues of the age through the establishment of a series of Communities. Firstly it showed that nationhood was not something that could be brushed aside lightly. Secondly it demonstrated that the solution to this kind of problem did not necessarily have to be a supranational one. When the EDC treaty was rejected, some inspired re-drafting of existing treaties allowed West Germany to raise its own army within NATO, an American-led military alliance between sovereign states. Far from being European and federalist, the answer on this occasion was Atlanticist and international. The chain of events that was supposed to produce a federation through the inescapable logic of things was broken.

After the failure of the EDC, it could therefore no longer be assumed that there was an irresistible impetus in European affairs driving forward a natural progression from problem to solution to unification. Nevertheless, in June 1955 representatives of the Coal and Steel Six met in Messina to relaunch the Community system. This time there was no special crisis to avert, no particular situation to save; simply the desire to do something "European" for its own sake. Whatever the result, it would not derive from the force of circumstances but from a spontaneous act of political will.

Two possible projects emerged. True to form, Monnet was thinking along the lines of supranational control of new sources of energy. Already, the development of nuclear power seemed to herald the end of the age of coal. Monnet therefore supported a European Atomic Energy Community (EAEC), which soon became known by the snappier name of "Euratom".

The other proposal, favoured by the three Benelux countries, started from the idea of a customs union.[10]

Instead of each country charging its own duties on goods entering its territory, the same tariffs would be applied by all members; in effect erecting a single customs barrier around the Six. Within that barrier, goods would circulate freely across the borders between member states in a Common Market. This shared economic space would be regulated on a supranational basis, making a European Economic Community (EEC).

Both proposals went forward, but of the two Monnet still leaned towards Euratom. This penchant was generally shared by his countrymen involved in the negotiations to bring the two new Communities to fruition. At one point when the negotiations seemed irretrievably bogged down, Monnet even considered abandoning the idea of a Common Market to concentrate on Euratom.[11]

In the event, it was the persistence of the German delegation that kept the Common Market alive. The key to its survival was the inclusion of a Common Agricultural Policy that would mostly benefit French farmers. The project to form a European Economic Community went forward on this basis, and the rest is

History. The famous Treaty of Rome signed in 1957 was in fact two treaties: one establishing the EEC and the other Euratom. It was, however, the EEC which stood the test of time, while Euratom and the original Coal and Steel Community faded into insignificance and were absorbed into what became known simply as the "European Community". In turn this formed the bedrock of the European Union.

The Common Market

The Treaty of Rome was thus a turning-point. It was the moment at which Europe as we understand it today really began to take shape. It also marked the beginning of the end for a conception of European unification through sectoral integration. Henceforth, Europe would be more a thing of commercial interests and market forces. 1957 therefore saw a divergence from the pure Monnet method. What remained, however, was Monnet's belief that once the process of unification was under way, things would work out alright in the end.

There was some reason for optimism. Although the EEC would be very different in character to the Coal and Steel Community, it was to have the same institutional structure that its supporters regarded as a federation in embryo. The most optimistic saw a future in which the Community institutions took on roles along the lines of the American political system. Thus, the European Parliament would become the equivalent of the House of Representatives, the Council of Ministers would mirror the Senate, and the European Commission would be Europe's version of the White House.[12]

The final destiny of the EEC as the United States of Europe was, however, underplayed by those who believed in it the most. One such was Edgar Faure, prime minister of France in 1955 and 1956. Looking back thirty years later, Faure recalled the care taken not to trumpet the historic nature of the launch of the EEC for fear of stirring up trouble at a delicate stage of Europe's evolution. Grand schemes were out of the question; success depended on the right mixture of effectiveness and discretion.[13] This meant framing any moves in a familiar format.

Faure and other enthusiasts were aware that the principles of the Community system and the operational requirements of a Common Market were somewhat at odds with each other. On the other hand, the Coal and Steel model was available off the shelf and would serve the purpose without arousing too much antipathy. Its recycling for use in the EEC did, however, depart from the rationale of enlightened intervention inherent in the Monnet method. Rather than applying supranational control to a situation that required it (or at least invited it), the Community system was now being used to create a new area of activity and organise its future growth and development. This shift to a "managerial" style of European integration deprived Monnet's machinery of its "functional" credentials as a force for unification.

Nevertheless, this change of use was adopted without qualms by the champions of the "ever closer union" promised in the preamble to the treaty establishing the EEC. Not that this strategy took them entirely into the realms of wishful thinking. There was already a precedent for economic integration paving the way to political union.

Until the nineteenth century, Germany had remained a patchwork of hundreds of statelets run in time-honoured fashion by princes from their castles. This came to an end at the Congress of Vienna in 1815 in the wake of the Napoleonic Wars. As part of a general European settlement, the Great Powers agreed a rationalization in the form of a German Confederation of thirty-nine states. This much was imposed by treaty, but the process which then took over and made Germany a single country by 1870 had its own internal dynamic driven in part by the establishment of a customs union between the states. If the removal of obstacles to trade could transform the fairy-tale Germany of the Brothers Grimm into an industrial and political colossus in one lifetime, what might it now do for Europe as a whole?

So much was reasonable. The method deviated from the view of European integration that placed more reliance on technocratic control, but that had in any case suffered a setback with the failure of the EDC. As an alternative strategy, the Common Market certainly had the benefit of relaunching Europe into the post-war era of global market forces. As a coherent vision of a continent reborn, however, it left an important question unanswered. What would happen if the European Economic Community created did not someday turn into the United States of Europe? Without a comprehensive plan for taking the process through to a political union, the project took on a degree of ambiguity that made the final outcome uncertain. To Jean François Deniau, a political insider close to these events, nobody could be sure if Spaak and company would succeed in using liberalism to build Europe, or if commercial interests would instead use Europe in the service of liberalism. Time alone would tell.[14]

TANGLED DESTINY

TWO

A Liberal Interpretation

A rude awakening

Over the final half of the twentieth century the EEC evolved by fits and starts to eventually produce the European Union, of which it remained the core. More countries joined, the internal market was cleared of the last non-tariff barriers to trade, and the euro was adopted as a common currency by many of the member states. The idea lingered, however, that this was not just further progress towards a businessmen's Europe but a vehicle for a broader conception of unity that gave the EU a political presence on the world stage and also offered a shared homeland to the people who lived and worked within its borders. All the same, that extra dimension still did not have the substance that a federation would have provided, while in contrast the economic aspects were part of everyday life.

So what had the Europe founded on trade and industry brought the ordinary citizen after more than forty years of development? What exactly did this sort of integration mean to the man and woman in the street? The opportunity to open these questions to debate came with the publication of a European Constitution in 2005. In view of a membership expanded to twenty-five countries, the Constitution was supposed to update the complicated raft of existing treaty provisions and rationalize them into one document. It was essentially a housekeeping exercise conducted in full public view and intended to let in some light and air to a subject that had become tangled in technicalities and obscured by jargon.

To come into force, the Constitution required ratification in all member states. In some cases this was done by vote in the national parliament. Germany ratified in this way. Other countries put the question to the electorate by means of a referendum. Spain ratified by this method with no problem. In France, however, the referendum produced the first rejection. This result was then repeated in the Netherlands, but it was the French vote that dealt the Constitution the killer blow. For a country that since the days of Jean Monnet had made Europe the central plank of its foreign policy, this was almost unthinkable. What had happened?

In one way, the outcome reflected a sour mood among the French people generally. The President, Jacques Chirac, had put all the authority of his office behind a plea for a Yes vote. There was thus an opportunity for the nation to send a message straight to the top. This is, of course, a risk with any referendum. However the question is phrased, the public may be tempted to read it as: "What do you think of the present government?". From this angle, the vote against the Constitution may be seen as a deliberate slap in the face for the French leadership. Nevertheless, Chirac was under no illusions about his standing in the country when he called the referendum. As President, he had the undisputed power to choose the option of ratification by parliament, where he had comfortable support in both houses. Clearly, even taking into account his own low popularity rating he had still calculated on a win for the Yes camp.

Obviously therefore, the No campaign managed to attract a larger section of the electorate to their side than had been anticipated. This swing was particularly marked among moderate left-wing voters. Crucially, the Socialist Party was itself split on the issue; the official party line was in favour of a Yes vote but the leadership faced a rebellion by a number of its prominent figures, including a former prime minister. These rebels joined ranks with a motley assortment of anti-capitalist parties and political organizations on the Extreme Left to decry the Constitution as a plot against the working class. On posters, in pamphlets, and across the floor in televised debates the most common accusation hurled at the Constitution was that it was "liberal". Often it was further denigrated for being liberal in an "Anglo-Saxon" sort of way.

Paradoxically, the British government of the day was desperate to wriggle out of its own referendum on the assumption that the vote would go against the Constitution. In this country it seemed that Britain was not European enough. Meanwhile in France, Europe was condemned for being too British.

Clearly, the attempt to define Europe for the new millennium was struggling with the ambiguity identified by Jean François Deniau years earlier. Was liberalism building Europe or was Europe building liberalism? Merely asking the question afresh cast doubt on the established order – France the role model, Britain the spoiler. It was easy to suggest to the French public that something was badly amiss and that the European ideal was being subverted. For French pro-Europeans, this was in fact nothing more than some very old pigeons coming home to roost. In 1957 discretion was the order of the day, and so little was done to explain that the Common Market was a radical departure from the thinking behind the Coal and Steel Community. To the politicians shaping events, one sort of integration was as good as another; as long as a unified Europe was the end result, it did not matter.

In France in 2005, suddenly it did, and as the pigeons came home the cat was among them. The ensuing commotion was enough to get the Constitution rejected. In Britain the promised referendum was cancelled and throughout the membership of the EU a "pause for reflection" was announced. An epic process of unification had run into the sand and nobody had anything useful to say about it. One thing was clear, however. The French vote had been against a conception of unity that was now seen as being too liberal. After so many years of building Europe on the basis of free movement of goods, labour and capital this raised the question of the fundamental nature of the whole project. If "liberal" is a term of abuse, there must be some confusion either in the way the word is being used or in the very foundations upon which the European Union is built. Clarification of this point is thus crucial to the question of Britain's place within the EU and also the position of Europe in the global economy.

Of course there are nuances of meaning between the French *"libéral"* and the English "liberal". Each carries its own cultural baggage and is understood in that context. The meaning in both languages has evolved along with the same changing world and the ideas within it. If the sense is not now identical, the difference itself may reveal something about the social, economic and political forces that have shaped Europe, and where that process leaves us today.

A sense of history

Obviously "liberal" is from the same root as "liberty", meaning freedom. As freedom or the lack of it may apply to a number of human activities, the term carries various connotations applicable to a range of lifestyle choices. Often the freedom of any one person has to be curtailed in the public interest. In some cases this is self-evident. For example, nobody can be free to choose on which side of the road he drives. Other aspects of human behaviour are less clear-cut and the tension between the rights of the individual and the needs of society has long been a rich field for study and comment. As western civilization developed into what it is today, great thinkers produced works on liberty that still grace the book-shelves, but originally the question was much less complex. In the first instance, there was simply the emergence of the idea that personal choice existed at all.

In the days of the feudal system the main employment was agriculture, and society was rigidly hierarchical. The peasant was his lord's man, the lord was the king's man, and the king reigned by the grace of God. Those who did not rule or till the soil were engaged in skilled trades that were passed down from father to son. Carpenter, Thatcher, Smith, the list of common English family names is evidence of the generation after generation that lived by these crafts. There was a chance in a million that someone of rare talent might rise above humble origins or find a new life as an adventurer of some sort, but as a general rule there were no career options.

Centuries passed and agriculture based on the manor house and its surrounding domain gave way to a different pattern of land use. Now farm work was more often paid labour that anyone could take or leave. As advancing technology gave rise to new professions, there were also alternative sources of employment in towns and cities. Eventually, where the old monarchical order failed to adapt to this new social mobility the result was unrest and upheaval. In France, the revolution of 1789 swept away an archaic system of preference and patronage that was stagnating in its own inefficiency. Wider horizons also encouraged new attitudes. By the time the Bastille fell, the British colonies in America had already turned the page on rule by a King half a world away in London.

On both sides of the Atlantic the pressure for change confronted the hereditary principle with the belief that the conduct of public affairs should favour opportunities for everyone, not just maintain the privileges of the few. The idea that men and women should have the chance to make their way in the world was thus inseparable from the spirit of free enterprise that made it possible. Liberty and commerce went hand-in-hand.

Thomas Paine, one of the most influential writers of the day, was involved in both the American War of Independence and the French Revolution. In his book of 1792, *The Rights of Man*, Paine argued that the normal operation of commercial exchange was a better framework for the dealings both of private persons and of nations than the policies of monarchs and their ministers.

> I have been an advocate for commerce, because I am a friend to its effects. It is a pacific system, operating to cordialize mankind, by rendering Nations, as well as individuals, useful to each other.[15]

Paine held out the vision of an end to war and the establishment of a universal civilization based on economic interdependence. Without the interests of kings and queens to accommodate, free men would exist in harmony with their fellows through mutually beneficial trade arrangements.

This view was later echoed by the most published French liberal thinker of his day. In a book of 1814, Benjamin Constant hailed the arrival of a new era in which commerce would replace war as the basis for international relations. Constant believed that a turning-point had been reached in world history. Once upon a time, a war might have added to the overall wealth of the winning side in land, slaves and tributes. In modern times, he argued, wealth is no longer seen in those terms, but as the fruits of industry and the leisure to enjoy them. From this angle, even a successful war must now invariably cost a nation more than it could ever bring by way of benefit.

Futhermore, for those engaged on the field of battle war was no longer the heroic business that it had once been. Sword-play and close combat no longer put one's fate in one's own hands. Modern artillery meant that survival was little more than a matter of chance. You lived or were blown to pieces. Courage was now merely a sort of resignation devoid of any sense of physical and moral development through action. For the individual, as for the nation, there was more to be gained by hard work.[16]

Early liberalism thus gave primacy to the economics of production and distribution at every level. According to this view, the interests of nations no longer clashed but overlapped in a worldwide continuum of supply and demand that formed the natural habitat of the human species. Left to itself, the system was self-regulating and required no crowned heads nor the heavy hand of their chancellors. Those days were passing and with them the narrow horizons of a rigid social structure. Freedom meant life in a global marketplace open to talent and energy.

Twenty years after the publication of Constant's book, another great French writer and traveller picked up the same theme. Alexis de Toqueville was already famous for his book *Democracy in America* when he journeyed around England and Ireland in 1835, recording his impressions and his thoughts in a journal. In Dublin on 7 July he drew out the link between liberty and commerce and cited England as an example. There he had observed a sense of freedom that expressed itself in dynamism, self-reliance and an eye to the main chance. He concluded that these attributes had done more to make England a great commercial power than the mere accident of being blessed with good ports and an abundance of coal and iron ore.[17]

De Toqueville saw, however, that the hustle and bustle of the modern world was not for the faint-hearted. With opportunities came risks and the need for initiative, perseverance and vigilance. The chance of success always carried with it the possibility of failure. Liberty came at this price.[18]

In the early part of the nineteenth century, a combination of self-help and free trade was becoming an important part of a political outlook developing under the name of "liberalism". It was recognised that leaving human lives to flourish or not in a great wide world awash with supply and demand would result in some casualties. Nevertheless, it was thought that the general principle was the right one. In a lecture to the Mercantile Library Association in Boston in 1844, the distinguished American thinker Ralph Waldo Emerson put matters into perspective:

> The philosopher and lover of man have much harm to say of trade; but the historian will see that trade was the principle of Liberty; that trade planted America and destroyed Feudalism; that it makes peace and keeps peace, and it will abolish slavery.[19]

In Europe and America alike, great minds thus concurred that because money made the world go round there was the prospect of freedom for all. In 1885 a towering symbol of that hope was erected on the shoreline of the country that most represented the idea that nobody is confined to the social condition in which they are born. This was the home of the American dream, the land of the self-made man. The monument to freedom that welcomed new arrivals was the Statue of Liberty: a gift from the people of France.

Us and Them

The iron-framed construction that made the Statue of Liberty possible was developed by Gustave Eiffel.

The tower that bears his name and gives Paris its most recognizable landmark was erected for the Universal Exhibition of 1889 as a demonstration of the latest French technology.

It was not only in civil engineering that France was a world leader at this time. In medicine, the work of Louis Pasteur was revolutionizing public health. In music, Fauré and Saint-Saëns were filling the gap left by the recently departed Bizet and Berlioz. Art was being redefined as the French impressionists produced stunning images that would retain their power for generations to come. With the twentieth century on the horizon, French cultural and intellectual life set the standard for other nations.

Yet, the publishing sensation in France for the year 1897 was a book examining the reasons for the "superiority of the Anglo-Saxons", by the sociologist and historian Edmond Demolins. This begins with the observation that in every corner of the globe there are people of Anglo-Saxon stock who are doing well for themselves.[20] The author contrasts this success with the poor performance of countries such as France, which hold down their colonies but do not populate nor transform them. In these cases power is vested in a rigid administrative and military elite, whereas the strength of the Anglo-Saxons is in the individual qualities that they take with them wherever they go.[21]

The idea that this amounts to a difference of French and English national character had been forcefully expressed in 1846 by the eminent French historian Jules Michelet. In his book *Le Peuple*, Michelet sees the two peoples as complete opposites and warns that to imitate something so alien would be the death of France. With bile practically dripping from the page, Michelet decries busy factories, loaded ships and full shops as poor stuff compared to the pride of being French.[22]

Forty years later, Demolins will have none of this. For him, Britain has moved with the times and France has not. He sees a natural progression from ancient to modern in the opportunity to pursue a personal destiny distinct from ties of caste and clan. It is an outgoing individualism that takes the British around the world. They do it not for national glory but for themselves, and the mother country benefits into the bargain. The money that makes the world go round is the product of a million pairs of hands going about their own business. Demolins illustrates the consequences by giving the number of ships passing through the Suez canal in one year – French: 160, German: 260, English: 2 262. [23]

The publication of these figures and the runaway success of the book preceded by a few months an incident that brought Britain and France to the brink of war. Britain's presence in Africa was along a north-south line from Cairo to Cape Town. A French force set off from Brazzaville in the west and headed east with the purpose of cutting that line by claiming territory on the Upper Nile. This arduous expedition took eighteen months and achieved its objective by setting up camp in the small town of Fashoda, where it was discovered by a British army under Kitchener returning victorious from Sudan. War was averted only when the government in Paris agreed to abandon the garrison.

Before this decision was taken, one of the French officers at Fashoda was sent to Paris to report. Transport as far as Cairo was provided by courtesy of the British. Leaving a special train that had carried him

200 miles across the Nubian Desert, the young captain broke his journey at Kitchener's base camp to take a steamer on the next stage of his journey. He was staggered by what he saw, which made Brazzaville seem pathetic by comparison. There were workshops for building railway wagons and assembling locomotives, a foundry, warehouses and a port full of ships discharging supplies of every type. This was nothing like the French style of showing the flag.

> The British way of doing things is perhaps not the sign of a delicate people: it is a feature of a strong people. The English march for profit, the French for glory. Honour to them is not what honour is to us; but honour is only a word, a convention that varies according to climate. They have the honour of practical people, we have the honour of dreamers. This one or that will produce admirable deeds to which the other cannot aspire, but when all is said and done the practical folk will have the fortune, to the dreamers will be left the honour![24]

This was precisely the prospect against which Demolins

was warning in his bestseller. He did not see the question purely in terms of the influence exercised by the British from their island home, but as the spread of an attitude of mind, an approach to life, liberty and economics that would create a modern world beyond France's reach or understanding. The question of how France should react remains the same today, but with a twist. On the front cover of the book that began the controversy is a map of the world with the "Anglo-Saxon" areas shaded red. North America is coloured in this way to signify that it forms part of a widespread civilization that is essentially British, or even English. Within half a century the situation would be reversed, with Britain increasingly seen as the European outpost of an America that runs the world according to the values of big business.

THREE

The Post-War World

Pax Americana

Britain's finest hour came in the first months of the Second World War when she stood alone against Nazi Germany and Imperial Japan. This act of defiance and determination made eventual victory possible but not without the support of the United States. When America finally entered the war, Winston Churchill famously said that he had his first good night's sleep since the beginning. Churchill's relief was well founded. When American industry was turned over to war work, the result was phenomenal as new methods of production combined with technical advances to supply equipment that performed better and was in use more quickly than ever before.

Or course all of this would have been in vain without the legions of new soldiers, sailors and airmen who risked their lives to take this material into one battle after another. Homage is also due to the astonishing courage and endurance of the Russian people who turned the Nazi tide on the eastern front. In Britain, science played its part with inventions such as radar, the jet engine and the electronic computer. All that said, the great success story of the Allied war effort was American manufacturing. The Liberty Ship, the Flying Fortress, the Jeep went though design and development, down the production line and out across the world in their hundreds and thousands with hardly a pause. The drawings were made, the factories hummed and the orders were completed. Capitalism went to war and won.

On the Upper Nile in 1897 Captain Baratier had ruefully observed that it was not so much the valour of her fighting forces that made Britain unbeatable, but the projection over distance of her massive industrial power. Fifty years later, British coal and iron were replaced by American oil and aluminium with the same effect. Wherever the Stars and Stripes flew it implied the economic means and the political will to get things done.

In 1947 the United States could have taken on the world again, whereas Britain was at the end of her strength in many ways, but especially economically and was only kept solvent by huge American loans. Europe was a devastated continent, with a manufacturing base, transport infrastructure and energy supplies all in ruins. Relations between the western powers and the former Russian ally were hardening into the frozen hostility of the Cold War. As a monolithic Soviet Bloc took shape in the east, an impoverished western Europe looked on uneasily.

The American response was Marshall Aid, through which the Unites States would give western Europe everything that was required for a full programme of post-war recovery. Broadly speaking, there were three reasons for this unprecedented offer of assistance. Firstly it was a generous gesture towards fellow human beings desperate for help. Secondly, it laid the foundations for a future export market. A Europe that was too poor to buy American goods was in nobody's interests. Thirdly, a general return to prosperity would undermine the appeal of the communist parties in the remaining democracies. This was the new world order, American style: freedom, humanity, and the chance to make a buck.

Like it or not, the future of western Europe lay in

finding a place in this world view. Firstly, West Germany had to benefit from Marshall Aid on equal terms and thereby regain the industrial pre-eminence that France had thought gone forever. As we have seen, the result was the Coal and Steel Community. Then, the need to support the USA against the communist bloc led to the attempt to form a European Defence Community. To some extent, these were vehicles for a conception of Europe that looked towards an eventual federation, but above all the action taken was shaped by the realities of the American age.

The new facts of life likewise coloured the decision to relaunch European integration through the medium of the Common Market. One of the prime movers in this project was the Belgian statesman Paul-Henri Spaak, who predicted that the old Europe of the history books would eventually be utterly outclassed economically and politically by the new American superpower. To Spaak's mind, a divided Europe would eventually be nothing but a ragbag of "underdeveloped countries" by comparison.[25] The first step to avoiding this fate was the creation of a single internal market to rival that in the United States. Whatever the future then held, it would not be an inevitable decline into economic backwardness.

This made sense from Spaak's point of view but was a difficult proposition to sell in France. From the early years of the nineteenth century, there had been a well-defined current of liberalism in French political thought that had its champions in such prominent figures as Benjamin Constant and Alexis de Toqueville. There is, however, a difference between liberal ideas in circulation and liberal policies in force. As Britain embraced the principle of free trade in the 1840s, France could not muster a consensus to follow suit due to the influence of vested interests in government circles. The argument was not all one way, but the last free trade tendencies were overcome towards the end of century by the minister whose name became a byword for protectionism, Jules Méline.[26] From the imposition of the "Méline tariff" in 1892, French industry entered a long period during which it came to rely on state intervention for survival instead of innovation and competitiveness.

French industry enjoyed this cosseted existence until shaken out of its torpor by the negotiations to set up the Common Market in 1957. The reaction was one of shock and horror. Used to a comfortable regime of import quotas, tariff barriers and government subsidies, French industrialists now began to feel like men "naked on a desolate plateau where an icy wind was blowing".[27] While there was nothing else on the table, few politicians would stand up in parliament and offer these unfortunates as a sacrifice to the greater European good. The package only became defensible with the addition of a Common Agricultural Policy that would benefit French farmers, an even more important section of society. This was enough to turn the page on an industrial policy carried over from the previous century. Spaak's vision prevailed and the Common Market was established as the basis of a new Europe for an era when the future was being shaped by global forces that consigned the steam age to History in every sense.

A Certain Idea of Europe

European integration could hardly fail to be a product of its times. In the post-war period there was a stark choice between capitalism and communism. The countries of western Europe chose capitalism and were therefore in the American camp. The means of unification reflected the need to operate within that system. No doubt, while their methods were dictated by circumstances, the architects of the Common Market also looked ahead to a time when the supranational principle they had included would be the seed from which a European federation would grow. That goal, however, remained to be realised. In the meantime, the European Economic Community began actually to take concrete form and exercise the functions laid out in black and white in the Treaty of Rome. There was thus a "real" Europe and an "imaginary" Europe. The latter was in the hopes and dreams of those who believed in it; the former was in the world of industry and commerce.

This was how matters stood in 1958 when Charles de Gaulle returned from the political wilderness to become the president of France. De Gaulle fervently believed in the glory of France as an independent power but he found his leadership constrained by two irritations. First and foremost he chaffed under the domination exerted by the United States through such organizations as NATO, the International Monetary Fund and the United Nations. For de Gaulle, these organizations served mostly as a cover for France's submission to American hegemony. He was also vehemently opposed to the principle of supranationality, which he regarded as nothing more than a "myth".[28] The EEC he could stand because the Common Agricultural Policy being put in place would benefit French farmers, but the "imaginary" Europe that went with it he rejected as stuff and nonsense.

These pet hates became connected in 1961. In that summer de Gaulle put forward his own conception of Europe based on relations between sovereign states. This was named the Fouchet Plan after the chairman of the committee that drafted its several versions. Although de Gaulle gave ground on one or two points, the plan was clearly intended to be the cuckoo in the EEC nest that would eventually usurp the functions of the Community institutions, leaving in place an intergovernmental rather than a supranational structure.[29]

Events took an interesting turn when, while the plan was still in the early stages of discussion, Britain applied for membership of the EEC. Trade with the

Commonwealth was diminishing in importance and Europe now seemed to offer the new markets that would revive a flagging economy. It was therefore the Common Market pure and simple that was the main attraction; British political circles and public opinion alike remained generally uncomfortable with the supranational principle and suspicious about where it might lead. It would be far better if any developments along those lines could be nipped in the bud. De Gaulle was thus aiming to rearrange Europe in a way that suited Britain very well.

The problem was that de Gaulle had absolutely no intention of allowing Britain to join. From his perspective, British membership would be a Trojan horse for the Americans to extend their influence into yet another international organization. It was clear to all concerned that he would in all probability oppose the British application.

This paradoxical stance did not play well with two smaller countries: the Netherlands and Belgium. Paul-Henri Spaak forcefully expressed the view that the moment had come when either the EEC could take a definite step towards a federation and reject the British candidature, or go down the Fouchet Plan route and welcome Britain into a Europe where she would be perfectly at home. The logic of this argument did not impress de Gaulle, who refused to be swayed. Spaak also stuck to his guns and so was more than anyone instrumental in the abandonment of the Fouchet Plan.[30]

As predicted, de Gaulle then used his veto to reject the British application. To this day it is not clear whether Spaak was really ready to give up his vision of Europe in exchange for British membership or if he was hoping to bounce de Gaulle into accepting the supranational principle in exchange for excluding Britain, and so reopen the way to a federation in the future. In the event, de Gaulle was prevented from using the Fouchet Plan to destroy that dream, and Britain was kept out of the Common Market for the time being. The end result was therefore that when Britain did eventually join in 1973 the old ambiguity between "real" and "imaginary" Europe still lingered.

By the time Britain became part of the Common Market, however, the Anglo-Saxons had already established a presence and were turning a profit. As in 1897 the phenomenon was the subject of a best-seller in France. This time the warning bell was rung by Jean-Jacques Servan-Schreiber with *The American Challenge*.[31] In this book, the author details the extraordinary amount of American investment that has poured into Europe since the Treaty of Rome. He is at pains to make the point, however, that this is not just a matter of so many millions of dollars spent. It is more to do with the methods employed.

Like Demolins in the previous century, Servan-Schreiber sees the strength of these Anglo-Saxons in a certain attitude and the organization that they bring to any venture. The strategy is to choose sectors that are identified by their advanced technology, rapid innovation, and high growth rate. It is not then necessary to pump in money from the mother company because the project is an attractive proposition for investors on the European markets and public funding aimed at job creation. Europe is the new Wild West, and the Americans prosper by understanding its potential better than the indigenous population and moving faster than the natives can react.[32]

In fact the Americans have grasped the logic of the

Common market better than the Europeans themselves. Open borders mean that a factory can be anywhere within the EEC, the actual location being decided by whatever advantages are offered by the host in terms of subsidies *et cetera*. If the purpose of the Treaty of Rome was to build a Europe in which business can thrive, it has succeeded brilliantly, but the Americans have been the first to recognize the possibilities.

Servan-Schreiber's book was written as a wake-up call for the politicians and businessmen of his day. The salient point for the purposes of this essay is that it portrays the early EEC as a huge opportunity open to any commercial organization with the imagination to seize the initiative. In short, it eloquently evokes an economic climate that is "liberal" by any standards. Moreover, American companies were thriving in those conditions. There is thus a case to be made that thirty-eight years before the French referendum of 2005, the EEC was already rife with Anglo-Saxon liberalism. That was the path down which the Treaty of Rome had taken European integration; there was no mystery about it.

As things started, so they continued. True, the idea

that Europe should be something more than the basic Common Market never quite went away and led to the proposal that what was already in place might be transformed into a European Union. This did not, however, call into question the operation of the existing mechanism of integration, founded on the principles of free-market capitalism. Nobody imagined that the European Union would replace the EEC; it would be the EEC plus whatever auxiliary functions or attributes were appended. The general underlying philosophy would remain economic liberalism.

This chimed with a growing trend among the member countries of the EEC to leave more to market forces, with a correspondingly reduced role for the state. Even traditional parties of the Left began to question the need for the commanding heights of the economy to be in public ownership. The last full-scale attempt to run a western European democracy according to the old socialist orthodoxy was in 1981, when François Mitterrand became president of France. For the next three years Mitterrand pursued an uncompromising programme that included the nationalization of five major industrial conglomerates, two finance companies and thirty-six banks. His government also legislated for a one hour reduction in the working week and extra paid holiday for all employees. The result was the nation's finances in tatters and the currency in free-fall. There was little choice but to make the U-turn that brought France back into the European fold of liberal economics.

There was no great outcry. France rejoined the course of European history that flowed from the Treaty of Rome, and that was that.[33] Furthermore, the Minister of Finance responsible later became President of the European Commission. In this post Jacques Delors pushed through the programme of changes that led to the completion of the Single Market in 1992. Delors himself proclaimed that the Single Market would provide a boost to companies and strengthen European competitiveness.[34] Significantly, the project also enjoyed the support of the British prime minister of the time, Margaret Thatcher, whose very name was synonymous with privatization, the profit motive and a winner-take-all business culture. There could hardly have been a clearer indication of what sort of Europe was under construction.

After the Wall

Of course, Jacques Delors was working in the tradition of those men and women who always believed that any sort of integration was a step in the right direction. In particular, Delors had in mind the early transformation of the new, improved EEC into a European Union. He was successful, and the Treaty of Maastricht establishing the EU was signed in February 1992. Whether or not this was indeed progress towards a European federation remained to be seen, but in the meantime, as always, there were real and immediate effects. The editorial in the French weekly *l'Express* for 11 September 1992 proclaimed that one of the virtues of Maastricht was that it would attach France solidly to the logic of liberalism and turn the country away from its traditional reliance on a strong state with a finger in every pie.[35] This article appeared the week before a referendum on the treaty. *L'Express* was founded by Servan-Schreiber in 1953 and always retained its generally liberal stance thereafter. If it was in favour of Maastricht, there was no secret why. Still, the referendum approved the treaty by 51% for, 49% against.

1992 was also the year of the first elections in a reunited Germany. This was a clear signal that the battle of ideologies that had shaped the latter half of the twentieth century was over. Soviet communism had collapsed and American capitalism had emerged the winner. The countries of the old eastern bloc were all eager to join the EU, not for more production targets and five year plans but for a taste of that same dream. This was the spirit of the age in an enlarging European Union. With the model apparently accepted across the continent, the Constitution of 2005 went so far as to state in black and white that one of the objectives of the EU was to promote a social market economy that was also "highly competitive".

In a sense, the EU Constitution was therefore part of the triumph of the West, which Francis Fukuyama famously dubbed "The End of History". In another way, it was the climax of a longer story in which the Soviet era was only an episode. From this perspective, the social mobility that came from the decline of monarchy blossomed with the advent of the machine age to form nineteenth century liberalism. This then became the creed by which the Anglo-Saxons lived and the tool with which they shaped the modern world. Communism was like a brief return to feudalism in its repression of the individual but could not hold its own in a world humming with free enterprise. In this story, the Europe of the Treaty of Rome had played its role as a champion of those values and shared the victory with the prototype single market on the other side of the Atlantic.

One thing that gives this reading of History a satisfying sense of roundness is the unifying thread provided by the work of Alexis de Toqueville. This was used to good effect by the department of the US government responsible for propaganda, the Office of War Information (OWI), which operated from 1942 to 1945. One of its publications was a book of extracts in the original French from de Toqueville's 1835 masterpiece *Democracy in America*. These include the passage in which the author predicts that one day America and Russia will each hold in its hands the destiny of half the world. The difference is that America will achieve this by hard work, whilst Russia will do it by force of arms. The genius of the former is in the operation of personal interest and the efforts of every individual, whilst the latter channels the strength of the whole society through its leader. One model is based on freedom, the other on servitude. Equality can lead one way or the other: to enlightenment, liberty and prosperity, or to barbarity, slavery and poverty.[36]

Although de Toqueville lived in the days of the tsars, his writing retained an unmistakable resonance in the middle of the twentieth century and, as a homage to liberalism, had an authority which no State Department propagandist could match. What effect the circulation of the OWI's digest had on its target readership is uncertain, but the intention was clear: to bring back to Europe the same message as in 1835. The lesson that de Toqueville learned on his travels is that liberal democracy represents not just freedom from arbitrary rule, but the chance to make a life in a world of commercial opportunities. In France today liberalism remains the idea that the fabric of society derives from the cumulative effect of individual initiative, rather than being a consequence of the operation of the State. There are none of the additional connotations that the word has collected in Britain or the USA. In French it still denotes government with a light touch and a *laisser-faire* economic régime. Essentially, it means that the market decides. It was opposition to this philosophy as a blueprint for Europe that produced the swing vote against the EU Constitution in May 2005.

TANGLED DESTINY

FOUR

A Time to Choose

The French exception

Viewed in historical context, the No vote in the French referendum appeared to turn the tide on the progress of an idea with a long pedigree into which European integration had tapped with the signing of the Treaty of Rome in 1957. After so many years of an economically liberal conception of European unity, what was now wrong with a document that attempted to put some order and transparency into what was a way of life for everyone within the borders of the Union?

It is not as if the construction of Europe was still taking place behind the backs of the French population. In 1992, the liberal weekly *l'Express* had welcomed the referendum on Maastricht not only because it was an opportunity to confirm Europe's progress in a direction of which the editorial team approved, but because it meant doing so openly rather than by the actions of a political elite. Until then France's leading role in European construction had relied on the discretion of the politicians and the docility of the electorate. After Maastricht, that was no longer the case, and the sort of Europe being built could no longer be in doubt.

Of course, in 2005 as in 1992 there were voters who would disagree with the idea of a Europe that was liberal in inspiration. The possibility that this might be a swing issue does not, however, seem to have been a concern for Jacques Chirac or his advisers. The political spectrum in France is wider than in Britain or the USA, and there is therefore always a chance that the main parties of Right or Left will see their supporters drain away outwards to the extremes. This is a risk that Chirac would have allowed for in calling the referendum.

From Chirac's point of view, the political landscape was thus no more complicated than usual. His own party was in the Gaullist tradition and retained a flavour of the nationalism that went back to Charles de Gaulle himself. Over the years, the party had become reconciled to a European future by regarding the integrated institutions as a kind of amplifier for France's influence in the world. More Europe thus meant more France, and a good level of support could be expected. In addition, the Gaullists had recently absorbed a large part of their nearest ally in the Centre: a party with a christian-democrat tradition and therefore pro-European as a matter of course.[37] The danger to the Right was in the form of two hard-line nationalist parties; one racist and xenophobic, and the other almost royalist in its attachment to traditional values.[38] Even allowing for the controversy surrounding Turkey's eventual membership of the EU, there was a reasonably calculable limit to the influence that these two organizations might manage to bring to bear.

In theory, the main party of the Left, the *Parti socialiste* (PS) should have been solidly behind the Constitution. The PS had crossed the Rubicon when François Mitterrand chose Europe over traditional socialist principles in his spectacular U-turn of 1983. After more than twenty years to digest the change, the socialists might have been expected to approve the text without too much soul-searching. This seemed to be confirmed in December 2004, when the leader of the PS, François Hollande, organized an internal vote to determine the official party line on the referendum. The result was an endorsement of Hollande's own preference for a Yes vote. In normal circumstances, party discipline would then have rallied members and sympathizers to the campaign in favour of the Constitution.

On paper, there were therefore sufficient votes from the main parties of both Right and Left to produce a positive outcome. In the event the Constitution was rejected by 45% for, 55% against. Exit polls indicated that Chirac's supporters had largely followed his example and voted Yes. On the other hand, six out of ten socialists had voted No despite the exhortations of the leadership.[39] It is on this ground that the battle for the Constitution was lost, and so from this perspective that the rejection must be understood.

To British and American observers, the French left-wing is remarkable for the influence exerted by the communist element. *The Parti communiste français* (PCF) is not just a marginal group of eccentrics but a major force in national politics. To the question "Are you now, or have you ever been, a communist?"

millions of French men and women would answer in the affirmative without thinking that it was anything to be ashamed of. In the 1950s, when in the USA Senator Joe McCarthy was ruining careers on the mere suspicion of communist sympathies, the PCF was the largest single party in the French parliament with 150 duly elected representatives of the people. Marxist-Leninist in ideology, the PCF always looked to Moscow for guidance. It used to be said that the PCF was neither to Right nor Left but to the east. Unsurprisingly, the party opposed European integration from the Coal and Steel Community onwards because the process consolidated member countries within a western frame of reference. Since the collapse of the Soviet Union the PCF has been an organization in search of a mission. In the post-Soviet era its natural ally is the Socialist Party, but this relationship tends to result in a blurring of the PCF's distinct identity and a slide towards irrelevance. This is rather resented by the die-hard faction of the party, for whom the ideal scenario would always be to take a stand on an issue that would rekindle its former glory and at the same time split the PS.

The situation is made more interesting by the existence on the Extreme Left of two more communist parties that are both Trotskyist in character. These are the *Ligue communiste révolutionnaire* (LCR) and *Lutte ouvrière* (LO). Neither have any time for European integration as we know it. Uncompromising, unreformed and unrepentant, they still strive for nothing less than the complete overthrow of capitalism.

In the past the three communist parties have been distrustful of each other. For the No campaign, however, they co-operated closely in a tactic that proved very effective. As leader of the PCF, Marie-George Buffet was entitled to play the prominent role in the coalition against the Constitution, but she in fact allowed a lot of the limelight to fall on Olivier Besancenot of the LCR. Marie-George Buffet is not a convincing communicator of ideas, and so mostly used her appearances to convey general solidarity with the ordinary people upon whom the wrong sort of Europe was being imposed. To Olivier Besancenot fell the task of handling the big televised debates. This was a good choice. His elfin features looked good on the screen, and as a postal worker he also enjoyed credibility and popular appeal. His greatest asset, however, was that he had clearly read the text of the Constitution and knew it back to front. On whichever point in the text the argument turned he could use it to convey his message. That message was the simple one that appeared on the posters of the communist newspaper *L'Humanité*: "Europe libérale – C'est NON".

This simple approach had the advantage that the Constitution itself allowed every opportunity for it to be used time and time again. Because the provisions of all previous treaties had been transposed into the new document, it had liberalism written all through it. It could hardly be otherwise after nearly fifty years of construction to that model. Page after page could be pointed to and quoted as proof that the Europe Union was indeed guilty of being liberal at heart. What had never been a secret was now presented as a betrayal, and the supposed victims were urged to throw out the Constitution before it set this evil in stone for all time.

This worked brilliantly because it was difficult for supporters of the Constitution to deny without falling into an elephant trap. The observation that there was nothing at all new about a liberal Europe risked bringing the response that there was in that case no need for another treaty. The off-the-shelf explanation was that a new text was needed to consolidate progress thus far towards an ever closer union of the European peoples. At this point the argument is lost by default because the two sides are no longer discussing the same thing, the No camp attacking "real" Europe while the Yes camp are defending "imaginary" Europe. One is protesting about a demonstrable fact, while the other is promising a better tomorrow.

Ironically, this recalls the line taken by apologists for Stalin who, confronted with evidence of his brutal methods that sent millions of innocents to the gulags, would reply "Never mind. It is worth it because we are building communism". While useful for rallying the dyed-in-the-wool faithful, this sort of logic is unlikely to win over any waverers who worry that they may be the next eggs into the omelette.

Also unlikely to make any converts among the vulnerable rank-and-file of the socialist electorate was the blunt assertion that the Europe Union needed the Constitution to *confirm* its liberal principles in order to compete with emerging players in the international market-place such as China and India. This raised the spectre of open borders being used by employers to drive down European labour costs. The prospect of seeing manufacturing jobs disappear to the low-wage countries that had recently joined the EU from the former eastern bloc did not encourage French workers to vote Yes. The counter-argument that under existing treaties industrial relocation could happen anyway only swelled the ranks of those inclined to vote No as a last-ditch protest.

In the run-up to the referendum, there was therefore from the Yes campaign no coherent message that would have broad appeal to the typical left-of-centre man or woman in the street. Conversely, the No campaign was simple, direct and focused. It said that this was a liberal Constitution, and therefore against the interests of wage-earners or any unemployed persons who hoped one day to earn a living.

The possibility of the moderate Left articulating a reasoned case for the Constitution was much reduced when certain high profile members of the Socialist Party broke ranks to join the No campaign. They, of course, claimed that they took this agonising decision out of conviction. This may or may not be true to some extent. The PS, like most French political parties of any size, is something of a vipers' nest. It would not be unusual for spite or ambition to inspire a manoeuvre of this sort, but that does not concern us here. Whatever the motivation, by their action these dissidents undoubtedly undermined the socialist position on the issue and reinforced the message coming from the Extreme Left that the Constitution was a fraud being perpetrated on ordinary, decent people.

Extensive media coverage of the subject actually made it more difficult to dispel this impression. It is a law of mass communication that it is easier to provoke fear and anger through repetition of a simple claim than to enlighten by a balanced treatment of a complex topic. For this reason television coverage favoured the tactics of the No campaign because their message had an uncluttered immediacy that came across well on air.

The anti-constitutionists also had the advantage when fielding questions taken live from members of the public around the country. Every household in

A Time to Choose

France had been sent a copy of the Constitution free of charge. Many must have been surprised to find that it was not at all the same sort of document as the French Constitution, which sets out in a clear and comprehensible fashion the principles upon which the country is run and how these are put into effect. The European Constitution was in fact an international treaty and so somewhat removed from the familiar framework of applicability. Confronting politicians in the TV studios, citizens strove to relate the turgid publication in their letter-boxes to matters closer to home. Typically, these would be quality of life issues such as the closure of a local post-office or school. Economic questions were also understandably on the level of individual employment prospects; for example a young person educated to diploma level who could only find work stacking shelves in a supermarket.

Everyone wanted to know how the Constitution would help them in these aspects of their everyday lives. The honest answer that it would make no difference at all was a gift for those arguing the case against. Any attempt by the other side to put things into perspective sounded evasive, or condescending, or both. Real people with real problems form the natural constituency of the *Parti socialiste* but it was unable to connect with their concerns on the human scale. This failure cannot be blamed entirely on the disarray caused by the defection of prominent figures to the No camp. Even among those who adhered to party policy there was no concerted effort to occupy an intellectual ground that could be defended on the key question of a Europe justifiably characterized as liberal. No amount of platitudes would substitute for a clear socialist view of what that meant for the French working class.

That kind of presence on the political terrain was vitally important but also very difficult to achieve. The message from the Extreme Left was unequivocal – if the Europe being built does not conform to a model that is left-wing in the French tradition, then it is the wrong sort of Europe. This point of view is obviously much easier to sell than the idea that perhaps the Left needs a new approach to the issues of the day in keeping with reality. It was precisely this shift in outlook that the PS had failed to develop. By the time of the referendum it was too late.

This policy void allowed the No campaign aimed at the socialist grassroots to attach to the referendum a sub-text about the preservation of the "French exception". The question was thereby transformed into a matter of resistance to the creeping generalization of an economic climate that was alien to French culture. The PS was mute on this subject because it had never formulated a credible response of its own. To the campaign of the anti-liberals there was therefore no countervailing voice of reason from the mainstream Left. The result was that a large section of society saw fit to repudiate the basic philosophy behind the Treaty of Rome.

Coming at a crucial juncture in the evolution of the EU, that movement had a significance beyond France and beyond the fateful day itself. Fifty-five percent of voters said No for a variety of reasons spanning the political spectrum, but it is apparent that the swing vote occurred on the Left as a protest against liberalism. The determining factor was the extra support that swelled the ranks of the five million or so communist sympathizers who would have been in the No camp as a matter of course. The Constitution became a dead letter for the whole of the EU because in France enough men and women of a moderate socialist disposition were convinced that it did not reflect a correct view of Europe, the world, and their own place in one and the other.

From this perspective, the failure to ratify the Constitution was the latest episode in a longer story about the nation and the individual in the wider scheme of things. France had withdrawn inwards while nineteenth century liberalism went around the globe as an Anglo-Saxon speciality that eventually became a medium for the immense economic power of the United States of America. The Common Market sought to emulate that success in the name of European unification; a process that seemed to be taken for granted until May 2005. In historical context, the result of the French referendum therefore takes on the character of a re-emergence of fundamental differences that stretch back long before the two world wars.

Of men and markets

In the broad sweep of History, the challenge from Soviet communism was but a brief interlude in the onward march of the liberal model, while French hostility survived to call into question the guiding principle of the European Union itself. This seems strange to say the least. If the French people no longer recognize themselves as part of the European project, the result is an identity crisis for both. With the future of the EU on hold, this is more than a minor nuisance to be blamed on French contrariness. Nor is it about sovereignty. Certainly we can catch glimpses of national interests and ancient rivalries going back to the dawn of modern times, but the underlying question, now as then, is about how we understand personal liberty in an age that belongs to money and machines.

Still, a world in which everything is available at a price is not necessarily dehumanizing. On the contrary, if goods and services are obtainable without the use of force, so much the better for mankind as a whole. As early as 1814 Benjamin Constant wrote that the civilized world was already too sophisticated to have anything to gain from war. In the years that followed this view was echoed by Tom Paine, Alexis de Toqueville and others but did not receive a full treatment until 1908 in *The Great Illusion* by Norman Angell. In this book, which was translated into more than twenty languages, the author demonstrates that war brings no material advantages but instead disrupts the pattern of economic activity that is of benefit to all. He gives the United States as an illustration:

> Where four hundred thousand Red Indians, divided into tiny nations perpetually fighting each other, starved, a hundred million modern Americans organized into one nation do not fight but live in plenty.[40]

Angell's book was a publishing phenomenon but did not prevent the Great War of 1914-1918. The author received the Nobel Prize for Peace in 1933 and brought out a new edition of *The Great Illusion* in 1938 before the outbreak of the Second World War. Again millions died and, as predicted, none of the survivors was any better off. Far from it. It was fifty years after Angell's example of the Red Indians first appeared on the page before the Europeans took the lesson to heart with the establishment of the Common Market.

A Time to Choose

As we have seen, this was not the strategy for European integration originally favoured by Jean Monnet and his supporters. Nevertheless, divergence from a method based on technocratic control was not inconsistent with the goal of peace and prosperity for everyone. The error was to embark upon the new path to unity almost by stealth without any determined attempt to enlighten the French public. The price for that omission was paid in May 2005.

Yet, in the intervening years, Europe had been transformed from the seething cauldron of bitterness and mistrust that had claimed so many lives for so long. To some extent, the No vote in the French referendum represented a failure to appreciate how that framework for pacific coexistence derives from free choice in an open market.

When Germany occupied France during the war years the only benefit to the ordinary soldier was in what he took by the threat of violence. For these pickings he had to be prepared to kill and risk being killed in return. Today, that soldier's children and grandchildren can have a bottle of French wine, a pound of cheese or any other product merely by purchasing it. Furthermore, thousands of German citizens now own holiday homes in the south of France. In a personal capacity they enjoy legal title to a piece of French territory. To take another example, the Dordogne region is known for its many old fortified towns or *bastides* dating back to the Hundred Years War with England. The concentration of British residents is now so high that the area is known humorously as "Dordogneshire".

The difference in both cases between now and then is in the concept of possession. The English archers and the German riflemen were risking their (very real) lives for a share in the (perfectly abstract) notion that their home country "owned" France. This is part of Angell's "great illusion". By comparison, the opportunity to obtain for oneself whatever is for sale anywhere opens the way to a more rational and ultimately more humane world.

Like it or not, the Common Market thus promotes peaceful coexistence through the medium of a more materialistic, more individualistic society. In the economic sense, the nation becomes irrelevant for a population of Europeans who are all consumers. This leaves a problem, however. A nation stops at its borders, as indeed does the European Union, but supply and demand permeate both. The question of what the state should do to interpose between its citizens and the great wide world therefore drifts upwards towards the level of the supranational institutions. That transfer is, however, far from complete in the perception of all Europeans. Here again, the difference in attitudes comes back to the historic divide between French and Anglo-Saxon ideas about the citizen and the State.

Old habits

For liberalism to flourish, it requires a culture of free enterprise and a government with a light touch. In these respects, Britain and France began to diverge well before the industrial revolution. The most famous document in British history is the Magna Carta, which in 1215 recognized the rights of the barons and freemen as opposed to those of the Crown, with the result that political power remained diffuse over the centuries. This was also true of France until power was drained away from the nobility and concentrated in the hands of the monarchy during the 1600s as a policy of the King's minister, Cardinal Richelieu, and his successor, Cardinal Mazarin. This latter was responsible for introducing Louis XIV to Jean-Baptiste Colbert, who developed the style of public administration that bears his name. The essence of Colbertism is protectionism plus State involvement in every aspect of commerce and industry. It was this combination of centralization and interventionism that set France apart from Britain in a way that was a subject of comment into the following century and beyond.

In 1734, Voltaire published his *Lettres philosophiques,* in which he drew a contrast between the top sections of society in the two countries.

> Which is the more valuable citizen, a French nobleman who can tell you exactly what time the King gets up and goes to bed, or an English merchant who gives orders to Surat and Cairo from his office, contributes to the happiness of the world and enriches his country?[41]

In 1747, Montesquieu, another towering figure in French literature, published his great work on politics

De l'esprit des lois. Like Voltaire, he saw that priorities were different across the Channel and noted that, while other countries obliged commercial interests to give way to political ones, in England it had always been the opposite.[42] Neither of these men of letters gives the impression that they find anything unsavoury in the British way of doing things. There is none of the vitriol that Jules Michelet would pour on the subject a century later.[43]

Thanks to Montesquieu and Voltaire there was therefore in France an awareness that economic life could go on without the machinery of the State extending into every corner. With the coming of the French Revolution in 1789 there was obviously an opportunity to dismantle the whole system but the character of the new regime depended on the outcome of a struggle between two rival factions. One side, the Girondins, leaned towards Voltaire's point of view. They looked for support more to the business community than to the revolutionary masses in Paris and imagined political power being dispersed among the members of an enlightened bourgeoisie. Their opponents, the Jacobins, were of a more totalitarian

85

tendency and believed in the virtues a strong, centralized State. To cut a long story short, the Jacobins won and in effect maintained France on the course set by Richelieu and Colbert in the days of the kings.[44]

Nothing is more revealing of the differences between British and French culture than the words that we borrow from the French language because the concept expressed has never required an English equivalent. A good example is the word "dirigisme", meaning just the sort of habitual and systematic State control that remains a feature of French political life even today and puts France at odds with the ethos of the European Union. From the 1960s onwards, succeeding governments have backed "national champions", that is to say large concerns that in terms of technology or market share have a world-class profile. Of course France is not alone in this. Even in Britain there are sometimes cases of the public purse being used to prop up ailing giants that have a prestige value. The difference is that in Britain this is a last-ditch option, whereas in France it is a conditioned reflex.

A good example occurred in March 2006. The

Italian company Enel launched a hostile takeover bid for the French energy group Suez. For the shareholders, this was an interesting proposition and looked likely to succeed. Immediately, the French government moved to bolster Suez by announcing the group's fusion with Gaz de France, of which the State owned 80%. This holding was to be reduced to something under 40%, effectively privatizing the company for the merger to go ahead and put the combined business out of the reach of Enel. The Italian government cried foul but could do very little about it. Typically, the whole manoeuvre was completed behind closed doors within five days. Such is the intermingling of political and industrial elites in France that the deal could go through on the nod and be announced in the name of "economic patriotism" without any sense of shame from those involved. The newspaper *Le Monde* came up with the equally snappy, and more apt, "capitalism of connivance" to describe the episode.[45] Nobody, however, was astonished to see the State intervene in this manner.

So much for big business and high finance, but that is only one side of the coin. Obviously, if French capitalism has that closeness to political power, French labour must have its own place in the same environment. There is thus a different perspective on what it means to be left-wing compared to how the matter is understood in countries with a more liberal tradition. In Britain, for example, the Left grew out of the Labour movement and so essentially defines an attitude of employee to employer. In France the Left still harks back to the Revolution and so expresses a relationship between citizen and State. In Britain the conflict of interests is in a horizontal plane between bosses and workers and is handled direct. In France the idea of class struggle means that both sides try to get as much as possible from the State. The power relationship is therefore essentially triangular.

In Britain, the trade unions first and foremost represent their members' interests through collective bargaining. In France the role of trade unions is to rally support for an ideology which they represent outside the workplace to the world at large. In Britain the working class looks to the government to provide the conditions in which the most can be wrung from the employers according to circumstances. In France, both sides expect the government to grant privileges that are set in stone for all time. This is the legacy of the Revolution. Where once the king bestowed his favours on the minority, now they are the right of all.

Of course the foregoing paragraphs are a simplification. As in all caricatures, the peculiar features are exaggerated to make the whole picture readily recognizable. A recent example illustrates the delicate balancing act required when it is from the State that all blessings flow.

French labour law (the *code du travail*) imposes an obligation on employers to go through an official administrative procedure before firing a worker. This makes companies reluctant to take on staff in response to increased demand because it is difficult to reduce the workforce if business then drops off. It is simpler to offer longer delivery times and risk the order going elsewhere, perhaps to an EU country with a more flexible regime. As a result it is particularly difficult for young people to break into the job market. Consequently France has an exceptionally high rate of youth unemployment, with all the attendant social problems.

In March 2006, the prime minister, Dominique de Villepin, rushed through a new law designed to alleviate the situation. This introduced a new type of contract, the CPE (*contrat première embauche*), available to a person under the age of 26 looking for a first job. The advantage to the employer was that anyone offered work under the terms of the new contract could, during the first two years, be released without going through the usual formalities. For French youth, it gave the chance of an entry into the world of work.

The reaction was one of outrage. In schools and universities students erected barricades and staged sit-ins. The streets were thronged with demonstrators and thick with the banners of the trade unions. Public sector workers came out in support and there were calls for a general strike. Amidst mounting protest, often violent, the country became ungovernable and a law that had been passed in due and proper form had to be hastily withdrawn.[46] To anyone unfamiliar with French politics, it was incomprehensible. In a country like Britain, it seems absolutely normal that a company might take on an employee to see how things work out between them. In France, this is an affront to human dignity unless the State is fully involved as a third party.

March 2006 was generally a month of unrest in France. While the energy market was being doctored for the sake of economic patriotism and the streets were full of the unemployed demanding a job for life or nothing at all, French wine producers were acting as highwaymen to prevent Italian and Spanish wines coming perfectly legally into the country. Again, this was not a direct attack on rival producers over the border. The fact that the television cameras were on hand when the tankers were stopped, the valves opened and the motorway flooded with wine is an indication that this was intended as another lesson for the government.

The salient point is that the protests about the CPE or imported wine carry the same message as the No campaign in the referendum on the Constitution. Basically, they call for the State to interpose between its citizens and an uncertain world in which market forces predominate. In effect a section of the Left in France is becoming increasingly defined by a search for a post-soviet consensus founded on an anti-liberal agenda. This group is not just composed of communists clinging to old certitudes. Naturally, there are hardliners who would still welcome the establishment of the dictatorship of the proletariat, but this faded dream does not provide focus or cohesion for a broad membership. Without a shared ideology, the core principle of the new movement is that things are no good as they stand and a different sort of world is possible. This is what mobilizes the *altermondialistes*.

Typical of these is José Bové, who campaigns against poor quality food and has been jailed for destroying fields of organically modified crops and for burning down a MacDonalds restaurant. In both cases there was an unmistakable element of anti-Americanism, the perception being that "made in the USA" means cheap and nasty rubbish foisted on consumers to line the pockets of shareholders and pay inflated bonuses to chief executives. This is the ground shared by the old Far Left, ecologists, small producers and the generally disillusioned. This is the new nexus of belief that forms the basis of an anti-liberal stance and a common platform of sorts.

It would be easy to dismiss this patchwork alliance as unrealistically utopian, wildly idealistic or simply nostalgic for the days when Marxism meant something. On the other hand, its challenge to the status quo succeeded in changing the course of European history and still awaits an answer. If Europe is not liberal, then what is it and how does it fit into the world today?

For the individual without power or influence the defining characteristic of the modern world is uncertainty. This is not a new phenomenon but the result of an evolution in society over the last century. Few ordinary people nowadays expect to be employed in the same line of work as their fathers and grandfathers. Sometimes it is a question of an ancient craft going into slow decline, but where the human worker serves the machine, the job can disappear almost overnight. For example, glass blowers and blacksmiths still survive as niche occupations but the telegraph operator and stoker have gone forever. Change therefore no longer occurs only from one generation to the next but may be sudden in application and brutal in effect. New materials and techniques can make years of experience worthless almost overnight, so that for large sections of the working class it is by no means certain that the skills they learn as school-leavers will support them until retirement.

There is, however, a positive aspect to this spasmodic reconfiguration of the job market. As new skills are called for, new openings are created for those who acquire them. It was this feature of the industrial revolution that encouraged a social mobility that chimed with the enterprising and opportunistic side of human nature and made liberalism a natural part of the spirit of the age. For those who could ride the breaking wave of innovation the future was full of possibilities. Of course, progress has always been less welcome for those left behind as was evidenced by the Luddites who banded together to smash newly introduced machinery in the early 1800s.

The Luddites were thinking of the type of livelihood that was disappearing. The greater significance, however, was in the nature of the new machine-minding employment that was coming. This meant not only that the workforce was at the mercy of new technological advances but also that the job could be done wherever the machines were installed. As long as this depended on water power the options were limited, but steam and then electricity meant that factories could be set up almost anywhere. The option then was to relocate to wherever in the world labour costs were lowest.

Today this is standard practice under what we now know as "globalization", but is by no means a new trend. In 1933, the French writer Paul Valéry asked what would become of Europe when, thanks to the efforts of the Europeans themselves, steel, paper, textiles, ceramics and everything else would be produced in Asia at unbeatable prices.[47]

In his book of 1897, Edmond Demolins, far from decrying this delocalization of production, already gives it as an example of the superiority of the Anglo-Saxons. He notes that if German industry can offer an item at a lower price because of the higher wages in England, the English manufacturer will not hesitate to switch production to "poorer countries". Demolins wishes that French industry and commerce would display the same flexibility.[48]

A hundred years later, attitudes remain polarized along much the same lines. In Britain the loss of jobs on any scale for whatever reason is always regarded as regrettable and is resisted as far as possible.

Nevertheless, if all attempts fail, the inevitable is usually accepted with resignation rather than horror. Time moves on for workers and companies alike. Some famous British brand names have gone forever while others have survived only by moving the bulk of their manufacturing abroad and maintaining a skeleton organization at home. Even the telephone call centres that once sugared the pill for areas in industrial decline are now more likely to be in India than on Tyneside. On the other hand, the old Austin Motors plant at Longbridge, once the flagship of the British automotive industry, was rescued from complete closure by a Chinese investor. In the global economy, capital flows this way and that, and the unemployment figures rise and fall in consequence.

In English this state of affairs is called "job insecurity" and is experienced as an unfortunate fact of life. In French it is *"précarité"*, which translates as "precariousness", and implies something demeaning and unnatural. Similar crossed perceptions coloured the debate on the European Constitution. The French weekly *Le Nouvel Observateur* noted that the British publication *The Economist* described the treaty as dirigiste and statist, while in France the very same text was being roundly condemned for the crime of liberalism.[49]

If this were merely an academic point at issue it would not matter. The problem is that we are supposed to be "building Europe". This is the familiar form of words with which, time and time again, French politicians and commentators have taunted the sceptical British. Yet in 2005 the French referendum undermined the very foundations upon which that construction had been pursued since 1957. Now there is a discrete silence on the subject but the question raised by the No vote is urgent. If the French do not want the sort of Europe that we have been working on for the best part of half a century, then what sort of Europe is actually now possible?

The difficulty is that the Common Market was established to make a space for Europe in the world as it exists, not as left-wing activists think it ought to be. The general public in France did not object at the time because the implications were adroitly played down, and in any case the economic outlook gave every cause for optimism. The situation now is less encouraging and the liberal template seems less attractive. This makes it easier to present the Anglo-Saxon model as a survival from the days of Charles Dickens, whereas in reality Europe needs to be understood within a broader picture of changing times. In that context, the evolution of nineteenth century liberalism into twenty-first century globalization is one side of the story, but the other side is a corresponding development of civil society away from that portrayed by the novelist. The real question is therefore about how well the progress of European unification reflects that second trend.

It is true that the essence of liberalism in the early days was very much "the free fox in the free hen-house". This was a culture of winners and losers with scant relief for those at the bottom of the heap. In his account of his visit to Manchester in 1835, Alexis de Toqueville describes in stomach-turning detail the squalid living conditions of the poorest inhabitants left to rot in a last refuge between misery and death. Foreign workers whose human needs are reduced "almost to those of a savage" provide a source of cheap labour and drive down wages for the native English. In this urban melting-pot, wealth and poverty, enlightenment and ignorance, civilization and barbarism exist side by side. Even in its outward appearance Manchester seems to be a higgledy-piggledy testament to the capricious and creative force of individualism. Everywhere is a celebration of human freedom. Nowhere is there any sign of the slow and continuous action of government.[50]

This, in a microcosm, was the rampant liberalism of the 1830s. Already, however, there were the first signs that raw capitalism would not be given free rein to blight the lives of the most vulnerable members of society. From the Factory Act of 1833 onwards, working conditions came increasingly under laws that were applied by government inspectors. In the long years that followed, further measures were introduced regarding health and safety, unemployment benefit and the whole panoply of state aids that today serve to protect ordinary citizens from the everyday misfortunes of modern life. Sometimes progress has been slow and something of an uphill struggle; for example the National Health Service did not come into being until 1948. Nevertheless, the trend in Britain and elsewhere has been to mitigate the risks inherent in a market economy with a counterbalancing degree of social provision. The sick are treated, the poor are educated, the homeless are housed.

It is these "bleeding heart" connotations that attach most readily to liberalism in Britain and the USA, whereas in France the word still has a "dark satanic" ring to it. The accusation that the European Constitution was "liberal" thus conveyed the idea of a return to the times of Dickens or Zola. As we have seen, given the history of European integration, the text was bound to be liberal in inspiration but this fact was reinforced by association with the name of the leading light in its preparation. As president of France from 1974 to 1981, Valéry Giscard d'Estaing had been instrumental in setting up the European Monetary System (EMS) and was well known for his liberal tendencies. An able politician with a reputation for intellectual rigour he made an ideal president of the international Convention that convened from 2002 to 2004 to draft the European Constitution. Nobody could have done a better job, but Giscard lacks the common touch and is generally regarded as rather aloof by the French public. Moreover he has always been suspected of pro-

British sympathies. Any attempt to accommodate the British point of view was therefore open to misinterpretation. It would, however, have been futile to produce a text that had absolutely no hope of being accepted in Britain.

In the circumstances it was easy for the No campaign to imply much about the finished document by occasionally referring to it as the Giscard Constitution. This would have been enough to provoke a knee-jerk reaction by those for whom Giscard was always an irritation because of his direct attacks on the holy cows of the old Left. In a statement of his fundamental principles published in 1976 Giscard was clear that a collectivist organization of everyday life was a retrograde conception of society. Furthermore, he opined that certain people who sang the praises of such a system would not tolerate it for an instant if it were applied to them.[51] Of course, events later proved that those eastern Europeans who were at the time living under such a system would themselves shake it off given the chance.

Giscard's position was one of enlightened liberalism. For him, the role of society was not to regiment the individual by shaping his or her mind, but to provide the conditions in which he or she could personally blossom.[52] There should be a safety-net of guaranteed security beyond which there is scope for initiative based on individual responsibility.[53] The fundamental precept of Giscard's philosophy is that there should be opportunities for all but pain for none. Nearly thirty years later, the debate in France on the European Constitution revolved around the question of accepting this as the guiding principle of life within the EU.

There was nothing new in this idea. From the outset, the developing Community system took account of the men and women who had to earn a living within its borders. The Treaty of Rome was not merely a businessmen's charter but contained a section giving workers the right to seek and accept employment anywhere within its geographical limits.[54] Another section on social provisions laid out a list of subjects on which the Commission would promote co-operation between member states. These included labour law, vocational training, social security, health and safety at work and collective bargaining. There was also a firm stipulation that member states must apply the principle that men and women should receive equal pay for equal work.[55]

In the following years that saw the Common Market develop into the European Union, every new legal text reinforced the socio-political element alongside the free market framework. As it did for the economic aspects, the 2005 Constitution consolidated these provisions with the latest additions into a coherent form. Article 3.3 sets out some of the objectives of the Union:

> The Union shall work for the sustainable development of Europe based on balanced economic growth, a social market economy, highly competitive and aiming at full employment and social progress...
> It shall combat social exclusion and discrimination, and shall promote social justice and protection, equality between women and men, solidarity between generations and protection of children's rights.

It might be thought that combining a highly competitive economy with full employment amounts to squaring the circle but, nevertheless, in black and white in a solemn treaty both objectives are given equal value.

There is a section on workers rights including: collective bargaining, strike action, protection against unjustified dismissal, decent working conditions, maximum working hours and paid leave.[56] Everything is later reiterated as part of the general provisions governing the policies and functioning of the Union:

> In defining and implementing the policies and actions referred to in this Part, the Union shall take into account requirements linked to the promotion of a high level of employment, the guarantee of adequate social protection, the fight against social exclusion, and a high level of education, training and protection of human health.[57]

By any reckoning, this does not condemn anyone to a life of poverty. On the other hand it does not promise everyone a job provided by the State. It is the sort of liberalism with a human face that would seem unremarkable in Britain and perhaps a little too soft-hearted in the USA. It offers the chance for everyone to make something of their own lives without the risk that any setback will see them in rags, starving in a filthy cellar.

Freedom and democracy

The title of Giscard's book of 1976 was *Démocratie française* (French democracy). In its basic meaning "democracy" is government by the people or their elected representatives. It does, however, carry the further connotation of a particular type of society based on freedom and equality. It implies not just the right to a vote but the right to a life.[58]

This connection has also evolved as part of a pattern of changing times beginning with the advent of the machine age. When Alexis de Toqueville made his journey around England in 1835, universal suffrage was still some years in the future. In England and Wales, the Reform Bill of 1832 had raised the total number of voters to 652 000. In France the situation was even further behind, with an electorate that hovered around 200 000 out of a population of thirty million. "Nineteenth century liberal democracy, in short, was everywhere constructed on the basis of a restricted property franchise".[59] That original form of liberal democracy broke down under the pressure of mass society into: communism, fascism and the modern western multiparty system.[60] Fascism was defeated and communism eventually collapsed. What then remained was a mass democracy for an age of mass communication, mass production and mass consumption.

The question is how exactly the EU fits into this modern world. When the latest draft of the European Constitution was presented to the European summit meeting in Salonika in June 2003, Giscard opened his press conference by quoting in ancient Greek, the words of Thucydides that headed the document he held aloft: "Our constitution ... is called a democracy because power is in the hands not of a minority but of the greatest number". This is, broadly speaking, true. In the early days of the European Economic Community, there was an undeniable "democratic deficit" that gradually diminished as the European Parliament gained in legitimacy and power. The European Constitution took this a stage further by extending the co-decision procedure and providing for more transparency in the deliberations of the Council of Ministers.[61] These latest institutional measures will of course not now be applied, but can the EU in any event have any political meaning in an age when democracy increasingly equates to gratification?

This broad area of enquiry has been explored with some interesting conclusions by the French political scientist Jean-Marie Guéhenno.[62] His analysis begins historically in the age of hardship when the height of ambition for the vast majority was to rise above the poverty line and stay there. Democracy then had little meaning in conditions where the only real power was in possession. Politics as we know it developed as the necessities of life became more readily obtainable through reliable and generalized means.

This heralded the advent of what Guéhenno refers to as the "institutional age", in which a politically organized society occupied a geographical space where production and demand, capital and labour generated the opportunities for acquisition. That area could be sub-divided as the region became part of the nation, and the nation part of the federation. In all cases, the formulation and exercise of political will was, and still is, an expression of civic solidarity at any particular level where priorities are fixed, decisions made and the general interest decided.

For Guéhenno, everything changes when economic activity and human mobility are no longer bound by the borders that define any political space. Membership of the community is then replaced by temporary alignments of interest backed by resources mobilized for the occasion. The solidarity of social consensus is exchanged for access to a shifting network of alliances on a larger scale. The "institutional" age gives way to the "relational" age. In this light, the debate about the future of Europe between nationalists and federalists is simplistic and ultimately fruitless. Sovereignty at either level is no longer relevant. The world no longer works like that.

From this point of view, the individual is, *de facto*, a part of the global economy as worker and consumer, while the nation-state and the European Union alike are by-passed. Both may still be tempted to react to specific circumstances after the event but have difficulty in providing a structural response to economic forces that are everywhere and nowhere.

A typical example involved the so-called "bra-wars" at the end of 2005 that saw cheap Chinese textiles flooding into the EU. European manufacturers could not compete at the prices offered and complained bitterly. In contrast, the European retailers who had actually placed the orders were desperate to get the goods onto their shelves. Customers sensed a bargain and were not inclined to buy the home-produced alternative at a higher price; in effect putting at risk the jobs of fellow Europeans in the clothing industry. Yet if those workers were made redundant they would have less to spend on whatever provided the livelihoods of their compatriots who had bought the Chinese garments. On the other hand, more jobs might also depend on contracts that European businesses were hoping to conclude with China through reciprocal trade arrangements. In the circumstances is it more "democratic" for the European Union to tell its citizens where to buy their tee-shirts or to let the market decide?

A similar question was raised in April 2006, when the French car manufacturer Peugeot announced the closure of its factory in Coventry, England, with the loss of thousands of jobs. If that production were transferred to another EU country, perhaps one of the low-wage former eastern bloc members, would that be in the "general interest" or can that not be determined at the European level? If that is so, where does it leave European democracy?

Moreover, what does "economic patriotism" mean on the European scale? Over many years the European steel industry survived by restructuring, merging and contracting. One of the results of this process was the Arcelor group, built on companies in France, Spain and Luxembourg. In January 2006, this was the subject of a hostile takeover bid from the Indian businessman Lakshmi Mittal. The reaction from the French government was one of outrage. Calls for protectionism and references to "French culture" were not at all well received in India, where the authorities had the means to disrupt French interests if they had so chosen. For all the bluster, however, neither France nor the EU could do anything to block the bid because the owner had British citizenship and Mittal Steel was registered in Holland. Legally it was therefore an internal European matter under the rules of the single market.

The success or failure of the bid therefore depended only on whether or not it was accepted by the Arcelor shareholders. Of those, a large proportion were not in continental Europe but were "Anglo-Saxon" pension funds.[63] It is factors such as these that determine the ownership of all companies, not tradition, prestige or public interest. When the British plasterboard giant BPB was taken over by the French St. Gobain, the outcome was seen as heavily influenced by hedge funds, which bought up a quarter of BPB shares.[64] Of course this could be seen as the formation of a "European champion", as could the acquisition of British Oxygen by the German company Linde, or The Body Shop by the French cosmetics firm L'Oréal. The same claim could not, however, be made about the takeover of Pilkington Glass by Nippon Sheet Glass.

To some extent, these are all evidence that British companies are more sanguine about takeovers than

French ones. Such an interpretation would certainly confirm an Anglo-Saxon willingness to let the market decide, with a consequent apolitical conception of Europe as a mere facilitator. Conversely, there remains in France a tradition that organization means the application of legitimate authority in the service of a particular view of life. At one end of the scale, the *altermondialistes* would use Europe as a base camp from which to change the world.[65] Others would look to the European Union, not to challenge globalization but for a strategy to live with it. In one case and the other, there is an expectation that the EU will be a proactive participant rather than just the medium through which the global economy pervades everything down to the habits and outlook of the individual.

When the French speak of liberalism, they have in mind something like the political doctrine associated with Margaret Thatcher, British prime minister from 1979 to 1990, who is often quoted as saying that there is "no such thing as society". Across the intervening centuries, Thatcherism is therefore in direct opposition to the view of Jean-Jacques Rousseau, who in 1726 deplored the idea that relations between human beings could be reduced to nothing more than the means of acquisition. His attitude in this regard is summed up by a passage on luxury.

> ... luxury is the effect of wealth, or makes it necessary. It corrupts both rich and poor, one by possession, the other by envy. It sells out the homeland to indolence and vanity. It deprives the State of its citizens to enslave them one to another, and all to opinion.[66]

For Rousseau, the danger is that a life based on the availability of commodities transforms vague wants into absolute needs, the satisfaction of which brings no real pleasure.[67] This is very much the modern world of mass marketing as seen by Guéhenno. The difference is that Rousseau finds it an unnatural degradation of the social contract, whereas Guéhenno accepts it as simply a fact of life. For him, the idea that the liberty to get what you want has to be organized in a political way belonged to a stage of our development that is now past and gone.[68]

From this point of view, a European Union devoid

of political content would represent both submission to mankind's global destiny and also the triumph of the Anglo-Saxons as seen from French left-wing circles. It is, however, unclear how the rejection of the Constitution can possibly reverse that trend. True, the No campaign has lent renewed credibility of a sort to the Far Left in France, but there is no realistic chance of actually turning back the clock by systematically demonizing anything that could possibly be characterized as *"libéral"*. It is small wonder that the debate on the future of Europe so often becomes a dialogue of the deaf.

This must always be a likelihood, however, as long as the EU remains no more than a collection of loose ends. To some extent these reflect the conditions in which the process of unification was begun by the "founding fathers". Moreover, those men were themselves as much a product of the times as the circumstances in which they found themselves. They hoped that any questions raised would be dealt with by the emergence of a political project to encompass the economic aspects at the new supranational level. Such a development would have placed European integration in the mainstream of a history that saw liberalism develop from a crude free-for-all into a mature political philosophy.

Certainly, the Anglo-Saxons long ago eagerly embraced the opportunities offered by mass production, the factory system and the mechanization of transport. Likewise, they were the first to suffer the associated alienation and inhumanity, but also led the way in building a consensus that accepted the dangers for the sake of the benefits. The result was change and uncertainty for the individual, but within a society founded on a democratic overview of what the limits were.

Jean Monnet was French by nationality but was very much at home in the Anglo-Saxon world and knew that not everything was left to the market. His Community System subscribed to that logic, but was installed in reverse order. First came the strict control of the Coal and Steel Community, followed by the liberalism of the Common Market, with the political framework expected to arrive in due course. That never happened in any way that would make real sense of citizenship at that level. The result is a pale imitation of the Anglo-Saxon liberalism that once offered scope for personal fulfilment through a philosophy of life that was economically risky but socially cohesive and politically self-aware.

It may be that this era is now gone forever. It is possible that Anglo-Saxon liberalism and the French exception have both already been overtaken by the new global model. From this angle, implementing the European Constitution would in any case have amounted to little more than "rearranging the deckchairs on the Titanic". We cannot yet know for certain. Europhiles revere Jean Monnet as a man with a vision that he put into effect. Yet even Monnet could not foresee what his own legacy would be. The preface to his memoirs is a short sentence that serves as his own testament: "We are not uniting States, we are uniting people".[69] In the end none of that may matter in quite the way he thought. Perhaps Monnet's real breakthrough was to see that you cannot build the future on the misunderstandings of the past. That was his lesson to France and Germany in 1950. It might serve just as well as a message to France and Britain today.

NOTES

1. National Archives. FO371/70530, C.2151. From Sir Oliver Harvey to Secretary of State. 20 February 1948. Marked MOST IMMEDIATE AND CONFIDENTIAL. Marked as seen by Bevin by a member of staff.

2. National Archives. FO371/70627, C.3746. Longford (AKA Frank Pakenham) to Secretary of State. 7 May 1948. Headed: "International Control of the Ruhr". Initialed as seen by Ernest Bevin.

3. National Archives. FO371/70530, C.9889. Vicount Hood to PH Dean, German Political Department, Foreign Office. 29 November 1948 Marked CONFIDENTIAL.

4. National Archives. FO371/70530, C.10578. From Sir Oliver Harvey to Sir William Strang, Foreign Office. 15 December 1948. Marked CONFIDENTIAL. There is a comment in Bevin's handwriting: "This is very important. I will discuss with Strang and Henderson. EB."

5. BULLEN, Roger & PELLY, M.E. (eds). *Documents on British Policy Overseas. Series II, Volume I.* Her Majesty's Stationery Office (London: 1986) p3.

6. Internet source www.federalunion.org.uk/archives/spinelli.shtml. Accessed 13.4.2004.

7. MONNET, Jean. *Mémoires*. Fayard (Paris: 1976) Ch 12

8. National Archives. T229/750. E.Roll to Sir Edmund Hall Patch. 1 July 1950. Headed: "Schuman Plan" and marked SECRET. Marjolin and Roll were both economists at the start of distinguished careers. They had already worked together on important projects and had become close friends. In their respective memoirs each pays tribute to the other's brilliance and professionalism. MARJOLIN, Robert. *Le travail d'une vie*. Robert Laffont (Paris: 1986) p196. ROLL, Eric. *Crowded Hours*. Faber & Faber (London: 1985) p55.

9. This was achieved by a peculiar device of parliamentary procedure known as *la question préalable* (the previous question). This is a motion that the original motion should no longer be put. The resulting vote of 319 for, 264 against, 41 abstentions was a vote against any further debate on the EDC and therefore the end of the matter. By any standards it was a shabby way to dispose of an important piece of business.

10. It is commonplace nowadays to use "Benelux" as a convenient abbreviation for Belgium, the Netherlands and Luxembourg. In fact Benelux was a customs union established between those countries in 1948. It is therefore a precursor to the Common Market.

11. DENIAU, Jean François. *L'Europe interdite*. Editions du Seuil (Paris: 1977) p13.

12. Ibid. p74.

13. FAURE, Edgar. *Les clés de l'avenir*. Lettres du Monde (Paris: 1988) p15.

14. DENIAU. op cit. p68.

15. FAST, Howard (ed). *The Selected Work of Tom Paine*. The Bodley Head (London: 1948) p228.

16. CONSTANT, Benjamin. *De l'esprit de conquête*. Ides et Calendes (Neuchâtel: 1945) pp24-29.

17. TOQUEVILLE, Alexis de. *Voyages en Angleterre et en Irlande*. Gallimard (Paris: 1967) p206.

18. Ibid. p205.

19. EMERSON, Ralph Waldo. *Nature and Other Miscellanies*. Oxford University Press in the series "The World's Classics". (Oxford: 1922) p266. "The Young American" – A lecture read before the Mercantile Library Association, Boston, February 7, 1844.

20. DEMOLINS, Edmond. *A quoi tient la supériorité des Anglo-Saxons*. Librairie de Paris. (Paris: 1897) Preface.

21. Ibid. pp322-327.

22. MICHELET, Jules. *Le peuple*. Flammarion (Paris: 1974) pp224-227.

23. DEMOLINS. op cit. Preface.

24. BARATIER (Général). *Fachoda: Souvenirs de la mission Marchand*. Grasset (Paris: 1941) p187. It is uncertain why this book was

published in occupied Paris during the Second World War, forty-three years after the events it describes. Possibly the intention was to evoke a time when France was humiliated by Britain. Certainly there is something of a sub-text to the effect that the British do not have quite the heroic sort of greatness that would merit their rank in the world. For example, the author relates how his hosts on the British steamer could talk of nothing but the latest gadget on board: a Sparklet for making soda to put in their whisky. The general tone is, however, not one of hostility but of bemusement and sneaking admiration.

25. "L'Europe et son unification". Address to a symposium in Geneva 9 September 1957. *L'Europe et le monde d'aujourd'hui: Textes des conférences et des entretiens organisés par les Rencontres Internationales de Genève 1957*. Editions de la Baconnière (Neuchâtel: 1958) p51. (With regard to note 13 above) At the round-table session the following day, the French delegate, Colette Audry, regretted the widespread lack of interest in European unification in her country, opining that the Treaty of Rome had been voted by members of parliament who did not really know or care what it was about. Spaak replied that it was a pity if MPs did not read treaties but great events often passed unnoticed at the time. He knew this because Louis XVI kept a private diary in which for 14 July 1789 he wrote "Today, nothing important". Ibid p233.

26. For a full treatment see: SMITH, Michael Stephen. *Tariff Reform in France 1860-1900: The Politics of Economic Interest.* Cornell University Press (Ithaca & London: 1980) passim.

27. MARJOLIN, Robert. op cit. (see note 8) p282.

28. Press conference at the Elysée Palace 28 October 1966. GAULLE, Charles de. *Discours et messages: Vers le terme, Janvier 1966–Avril 1969*. Plon (Paris: 1970) p98. De Gaulle thus had a different view of American hegemony and a European response to it compared to that of Paul-Henri Spaak (note 25, above). These contrasting conceptions were never quite resolved and contribute to the ambivalent nature of the EU today. For a contemporary analysis see: CALLEO., David P. *Europe's Future: The Grand Alternatives*. Hodder & Stoughton (London: 1965) passim.

29. For a concise account see: PATTISON DE MENIL, Lois. *Who Speaks for Europe?: The Vision of Charles de Gaulle*. Weidenfeld and Nicolson) London: 1977. Chapter 4 passim and appendices 2 and 3.

30. FAURE, Edgar. *L'année politique 1962* (Introduction). Quoted in: DUPEUX, Georges. *La France de 1945 à 1965*. Armand Colin (Paris: 1969) p320.

31. SERVAN-SCHREIBER, Jean-Jacques. *Le défi américain*. Denoël (Paris: 1967).

32. Ibid. pp24-30.

33. According to Hubert Védrine, Mitterrand's diplomatic adviser, the president knew that he had no real choice but deliberately kept the poltical aspects low key. In particular he masked the importance of the U-turn by not re-shuffling the government as soon as the decision was taken. "France: le piano ou le tabouret?". Interview with Hubert Védrine in *Le Débat*, number

95, May-August 1997. p169. Gallimard (Paris). In his memoirs Védrine puts a slightly different complexion on matters by relating simply how Mitterrand took the decision alone and then carefully prepared the ground for the new policy. VEDRINE, Hubert. *Les mondes de François Mitterrand.* Fayard (Paris: 1996) p295. Mitterrand's economic adviser, Jacques Attali, recalls that it was firm opposition by the prime minister, Pierre Mauroy, and the minister of finance, Jacques Delors, to the president's inclination to let the franc drop out of the European Monetary System that forced the re-think in mid March 1983. Mauroy went so far as to say that if the franc were allowed to float, France would become nothing more than a "huge Portugal". ATTALI, Jacques. *Verbatim 1. Première partie,* 1981-1983. Fayard-Livres de Poche (Paris: 1993) pp617-622.

34. In the foreword to an EEC public information booklet: *Un grand marché sans frontières.* Office des publications officielles des Communautés européennes (Luxembourg: 1988).

35. Editorial by Yann de l'Ecotais

36. TOQUEVILLE. *De la Démocratie en Amérique (Extraits).* Avec une préface par Gilbert Chinard. L'Office de l'Information de Guerre des Etats-Unis. No date of publication but bears the reference number US 850 FR.

37. Chirac's party, the *Rassemblement pour la République* (RPR), merged with elements of the *Union pour la démocratie française* (UDF) to form the UMP in 2002. For the purposes of the election campaign that year the initials stood for *Union pour la majorité présidentielle,* but were later recycled to mean *Union pour un*

NOTES

mouvement populaire.

38. Respectively the *Front national* and the *Mouvement pour la France*. There is also a splinter party that split from the FN, the *Mouvement national républicain.*

39. Le Monde. 31 May 2005.

40. ANGELL, Norman. *The Great Illusion – Now.* Penguin (Harmondsworth: 1938) p206. This edition contains an abridged version of the original text, together with new material.

41. Borrowed from MITFORD, Nancy. *Voltaire in Love.* Hamish Hamilton (London:1957) p37. The original French is in VOLTAIRE. *Lettres philosophiques.* Garnier-Flammarion (Paris: 1964) p67.

42. Part 4, book XX, para 7. MONTESQUIEU. *Oeuvres complètes.* Editions du Seuil (Paris: 1964) p652.

43. Above.

44. This was not just a case of losing a battle of ideologies. The Girondins were to a large extent victims of their own tactical errors and were outmanoeuvered.

45. *Le Monde.* 11 March 2006. "Le capitalisme de connivence". Laurent Mauduit.

46. The law was fast-tracked through parliament using Article 49.3 of the French constitution. The intention seems to have been

to implement it with immediate effect so that any benefits would become apparent before the presidential elections in 2007 and the credit could be claimed by Dominique de Villepin to improve his chances as a candidate. From this point of view the manoeuvre was a deplorable abuse of procedure in the service of personal ambition. Nevertheless, it was perfectly constitutional and did not necessarily mean that the measure bulldozed through was a bad one. On the contrary, it was clearly expected to be successful, otherwise it would not redound to de Villepin's glory.

47. VALERY, Paul. *Regards sur le monde actuel.* Librairie Stock (Paris: 1933) p44. *Considérez un peu ce qu'il adviendra de l'Europe quand il existera par ses soins en Asie, deux douzaines de Creusot ou d'Essen, de Manchester ou de Roubaix, quand l'acier, la soie, le papier, les produits chimiques, les étoffes, la céramique et le reste y seront produits en quantités écrasantes, à des prix invincibles, par une population qui est la plus sobre et la plus nombreuse du monde, favorisée dans son accroissement par l'introduction des pratiques de l'hygiène.*

48. DEMOLINS. op cit, preface pxii.

49. *Le nouvel Observateur.* No. 2117. 2-8 June 2005. p52. Article by Laurent Joffrin.

50. Op cit. pp185-191. Interestingly, the author makes a point of contrasting these appalling conditions with the much better situation in Birmingham. The capital of the Midlands is dirty, noisy and crowded but is a city of enterprise and small workshops, whereas Manchester is given over to large, de-humanizing textile mills. Rather than communal dwellings, the inhabitants of Birmingham tend to live in houses occupied by a single

family. Birmingham has more toilets and the streets are properly paved.

51. GISCARD D'ESTAING, Valéry. *Démocratie française.* Fayard (Paris: 1976) p73.

52. Ibid p73. *Le rôle de la société n'est pas d'enrégimenter l'individu pour façonner son esprit, mais au contraire, de le libérer pour faciliter son épanouissement.*

53. Ibid. p75.

54. Articles 48-58.

55. Articles 117-122

56. Part II, Title IV, passim.

57. Part III, Title I, Article III-117.

58. Of course, during the Soviet era it was commonplace for a communist dictatorship to give itself the airs of a People's Democratic Republic. There was not, however, the freedom of opportunity that would generally be associated with the term in the western world.

59. BARRACLOUGH, Geoffrey. *An Introduction to Contemporary History.* Penguin (Harmondsworth: 1964) p127.

60. Ibid. p129.

61. For a brief overview of the operations of the institutions of the EU see: WOODHOUSE, Roger. *Thinking about Europe.* Thumbnail Publications (Sutton Coldfield: 2005) Ch2. For a more detailed account see one of the standard texts, for example: BOMBERG, Elizabeth & STUBB, Alexander (eds). *The European Union: How Does It Work?* Oxford University Press (Oxford: 2003), or: NUGENT, Neil. *The Government and Politics of the European Union.* Palgrave Macmillan (Basingstoke: 2003). There is also a range of information leaflets by the Office for Official Publications of the European Communities and a useful Web portal: www.europa.eu.int.

62. What follows is freely adapted from: GUEHENNO, Jean-Marie. *La fin de la démocratie.* Flammarion (Paris: 1993) passim.

63. *Le Monde* 31 January 2006. Interview with Guy Dollé, CEO of Arcelor. *Le Monde* 6 February 2006. Article by Eric Le Boucher.

64. Financial page of *The Guardian* 7 March 2006. Article by Terry Macalister and David Gow.

65. The various *altermondialistes* groups have a common point of contact in Attac, originally a think-tank but now taking more of a coordinating role.

66. ROUSSEAU, Jean-Jacques. *Du contrat social.* Flammarion (Paris: 1992) p96. ...*le luxe est l'effet des richesses, ou il les rend nécessaires; il corrompt à la fois le riche et le pauvre, l'un par la possession, l'autre par la convoitise; il vend la patrie à la mollesse, à la vanité; il ôte à l'Etat tous ses citoyens pour les asservir les uns aux autres, et tous à l'opinion.*

Notes

67. ROUSSEAU, Jean-Jacques. *De l'inégalité parmis les hommes.* Editions Sociales in the series "Les classiques du peuple" (Paris: 1965) pp113,114. *Car, outre qu'ils continuèrent ainsi à s'amolir le corps et l'esprit, ces commodités ayant par l'habitude perdu presque tout leur agrément, et étant en même temps dégénérés en de vrais besoins, la privation en devint beaucoup plus cruelle que la possession n'en était douce; et l'on était malheureux de les perdre, sans être heureux de les posséder.*

68. Op cit. p14.

69. *Nous ne coalisons pas des Etats, nous unissons des hommes.*

By the same author:

Thinking about Europe
Thumbnail Publications
ISBN 0-9550223-0-4

British Policy towards France 1945-51
Macmillan
ISBN 0-333-63737-2
(USA: St Martins Press ISBN 0-312-12489-9)